W9-DCA-280

# NEW COUNTRY
## TODAY'S BRIGHTEST STARS

# NEW COUNTRY
## TODAY'S BRIGHTEST STARS

### RICK MARSCHALL

SMITHMARK

# Contents

Copyright © 1993 Brompton Books Corp.

All rights reserved. No part of this publication may be reproduced, stored in a retrieval system or transmitted in any form by any means, electronic, mechanical, photocopying or otherwise, without first obtaining written permission of the copyright owner.

This edition published in 1993
by SMITHMARK Publishers Inc.,
16 East 32nd Street
New York, New York 10016.

SMITHMARK books are available for bulk purchase for sales promotion and premium use. For details write or telephone the Manager of Special Sales, SMITHMARK Publishers Inc., 16 East 32nd Street, New York, NY 10016. (212) 532-6600.

Produced by Brompton Books Corp.,
15 Sherwood Place,
Greenwich, CT 06830.

ISBN 0-8317-6307-8

Printed in Hong Kong

10 9 8 7 6 5 4 3 2 1

*Left: Randy Travis maintains the best of country music's traditions. His Storms of Life was the first-ever in country music to go platinum as a debut album.*

*Page 1: With his trademark hat and straightforward style, Alan Jackson has been a star since his debut album in 1990.*

*Page 2: One of New Country's brightest stars, Lorrie Morgan conveys a depth and sensitivity in her music.*

**Acknowledgments**

Many people have helped in the preparation of *New Country*, assisting my constant research and contacts in this ever-changing field. First thanks go to Del DeMontreaux, Music Director and program host of WYNY in New York, America's most-listened-to country station. His advice and assistance were invaluable. We both were born in New York City – once upon a time needing our visas stamped to enter country music realms – and I'd like to think that I've been able to adopt a portion of the real enthusiasm and sensitivity for country music that Del has.

Thanks also to Ted Marschall; to Kevin Erickson, Bryan Switzer, Chuck Thagard, Tom McBee, Teddi Bonadese, Sue Austin, Chris Michaels, Rick Hughes, Dale Turner, Kim Fowler and John T. Davis.

The publisher would also like to thank the following people who have helped in the preparation of this book: Barbara Thrasher, who edited it; Elizabeth Miles Montgomery, who did the picture research; Adrian Hodgkins, who designed it; and Jennifer Cross, who prepared the index.

# Foreword

Back in 1973 finances at WHN Radio in New York City indicated there was need for a change. Ratings were poor with the pop format at the time, and a research project pointed toward country music as the likely direction to a successful revenue-producing radio station. So on February 26, 1973, WHN became New York City's first full-time country music station, with George Jones leading off with the "The Race is On."

And what a race it's been! There were some on staff at the time who decided country wasn't for them, and left. Some stood firm, anticipating the format's demise within a few months, when we would switch to what they felt would be a more appropriate format for New York City. And there were others, like myself, who believed we really had a shot.

Nashville could not have been more pleased. Cooperation from the country music community was enormous. Boxes of albums were shipped in from all the record companies, artists went into Nashville studios to record greetings, welcoming us to the family. It seemed that every day someone was flying in for a visit. Conway Twitty, Merle Haggard, Johnny Cash, Loretta Lynn, Dolly Parton, Mel Tillis, Willie Nelson – they all came to lend their support. I really sensed a genuineness about these very special people that went beyond "doing the right thing."

Once the music hit the air, the next question was: would anyone really listen? Boy, were we shocked! They listened, all right, incessantly. Suddenly we had thousands of program directors. Everyone had an opinion, and everyone felt the need to express it. Local country music associations were formed. Country music clubs were springing up everywhere. Where did these people come from? Artists were being booked into the New York area and selling out shows regularly. The growth of the WHN audience was phenomenal. Steadily we were becoming one of New York's most successful adult radio stations, peaking at number two in the late '70s, with a weekly audience in excess of 1.4 million people.

But competition in the new format brought declining ratings in the '80s. WHN gave up the format in 1987 when WYNY, a New York City FM station, took it over. Still, ratings remained at a stagnant level, and growth just wasn't happening. The question was: why?

Well, looking back, maybe it was the music itself. Perhaps it had not grown with the times. Perhaps it was not meeting the needs of today's country music fan, and it definitely was not bringing new fans into the format. The Nashville music community collectively figured out it was time to open the doors and let some new artists in. Some of country music's finest songwriters suddenly had record deals, and soon had hit songs and new careers. Talent searches began beyond the confines of Music City. The term "new artist" now seems to precede most of the introductions in country radio today. Country music is hotter than ever, and the new artists whose influences go beyond the confines of country music are undoubtedly the reason.

Today at WYNY we're known as "The New Country 103.5," because country music truly is new. The influences I mentioned have helped to bend and shape the music in many different directions. We continue to play the traditionalists, since they pioneered the format and will always remain the base that uniquely defines our music. In addition, a whole crop of "new traditionalists" have arrived on the scene. Heavily influenced by the early stars of country music, they bring a freshness to our sound by incorporating modern instrumentation, enhanced by state-of-the-art recording techniques. Added to this mix are today's contemporary country artists, who incorporate the varied sounds of pop, rock and soul, attracting a whole new audience of country listeners. This unique combination has given country music a truly new sound, and has brought hoards of new fans of all ages to country radio, concert halls and dance clubs around the world.

Thus the need for Rick Marschall's book. It's about today. It's about the "New Country." In 1985 Rick's *The Encyclopedia of Country & Western Music* chronicled the great artists who brought us to the dance . . . and what a dance it's been!

The excitement is back! As an air personality and music director for WYNY, it's a very satisfying time for me personally. There are many of us who can say in the immortal words of Barbara Mandrell: "We were country when country wasn't cool," but boy, is it cool to be country today!

DEL DEMONTREAUX

# Introduction

Country music is really not one type of music; even country western is more than two types. When Jimmie Rodgers and the Carter Family both recorded audition waxes in the little town of Bristol, Tennessee, in 1927, they each started separate but related traditions in country music. Jimmie Rodgers was father to country blues, honky-tonk, hard-life and hard-time lyrics. The Carter Family saw vocal ensembles, gospel music, sentimental story songs and bluegrass spring from their music. But they both inherited, combined and amalgamated earlier traditions: black blues, jazz, cowboy songs and ethnic influences in Rodgers's case; mountain music, shape-note religious songs, and English/Scottish/Irish dance tunes in the Carters' case. And through the years there were many more grafts onto the country music tree: folk music, western swing, cowboy songs, rock 'n' roll (a true case of cross-pollination), country gospel, bluegrass and bluegrass fusion, honky-tonk, uptown country and southern rock. But one graft never took: pop music.

Many country songs crossed over into pop, including the hardest of hard-core lyrics by Hank Williams and Floyd Tillman. But things seldom worked in the opposite direction. The reasons are surely as sociological as musical: The lyrics, themes and basic appeal of country are somehow antithetical to the same elements in pop music. It goes beyond rural vs. urban, basic vs. sophisticated and roots vs. gloss, although those factors are important. There is a basic honesty in country music that underpins its instrumentations and lyrics. It is an honesty that deals unashamedly with high and low themes – praising God and dealing with temptations, writing about frank emotions and singing about everyday disappointments, love songs with unhappy endings, life songs that despair yet hope. Country does not claim to corner the market – many other musical forms from high opera to low blues deal with these feelings – but pop music has always seemed too glossy.

But that didn't stop executives and some artists from trying to transform traditional country to pop country. From the mid-1970s to the mid-1980s there was a determined effort to make this crossover. Was it engineered from New York and Los Angeles? If so, Nashville executives were willing accomplices in the effort to change the sound of country music. There was a precedent: Starting in the late 1950s, the "Nashville Sound" had come closest to this hijacking, and there had been opp-

Left: *The father of modern country music, Hank Williams. Despite his innovations he relied on traditional country forms like the blue yodel.*

Bottom: *The continuum in a "family portrait" (l to r): Randy Travis, George Jones, Mark Chestnutt.*

sition to its string arrangements and lounge-singer voices in spite of its apparent commercial success. (Chet Atkins, architect of this detour, once jingled the change in his pocket and said, "Hear that? *That's* the Nashville Sound.")

But in the '70s and '80s it seemed that all tradition was out the window. Lyrics changed, artists were packaged differently, the soul was out of country music. It became a mystery why the industry still called it country music. Of course one other thing changed: sales of country music records plummeted. So a turn away from the pop infestation seemed inevitable, if for no other reason than business. Still it was a long time in returning.

But traditional country never totally went away. Artists like George Jones continued the modes of the '40s and '50s. Merle Haggard was new and innovative but was squarely in the Lefty Frizzell tradition. Hank Williams was still revered by many, not the least of whom was Bochephus, his son Hank Jr.,

who covered many of Hank Sr.'s hits. Moe Bandy maintained Texas honky-tonk traditions. The Statler Brothers represented the old sounds of harmony singing and sentimental lyrics. There were pockets of interest in bluegrass and Texas jazz and gospel, but they were drowned out of the larger stage by lush violin and brass sections.

There were also protests by country traditionalists who wouldn't go away: George Jones was a prime mover in the basics-oriented ACE, the Association of Country Entertainers. Roy Acuff, the King of Country Music, was asked to be a presenter to Australian pop singer Olivia Newton-John as Country Music Association Female Vocalist of the Year in 1974 (she didn't even attend the ceremonies), and he pretended to have trouble just pronouncing her name. Merle Haggard kept some flames lit by producing tribute albums to Jimmie Rodgers and Bob Wills; he educated a new generation in the face of country pop.

In spite of the stifling imposition of pop sounds, and probably due in large part to the efforts of the purists, a new generation was indeed being educated, deciding what to reject and what to embrace. They discovered much that was good in the tried and true forms. They respected the heritage. They realized that there was a lot of quality to emulate. They were called "new traditionalists." They are New Country.

The formative talents in country music's history are still the standards by which contemporary artists measure themselves and draw inspiration. Jimmie Rodgers, the Blue Yodeler, the Singing Brakeman, defined many of the themes and sounds of loneliness and joy that comprise country's basic preoccupations. Bill Monroe sang mountain music for years before he fashioned a unique instrumental ensemble and infused it with intensity and improvisation, giving birth to bluegrass. Bob Wills

took the instruments of the native and ethnic Southwest and fused traditional forms with swing-era jazz to give us western swing. Hank Williams yodeled in Jimmie Rodgers fashion and, tragically, similarly died young; but like the Singing Brakeman he breathed life into a form by creating a quality body of individual work, and he directly inspired honky-tonk and early rock 'n' roll. Lefty Frizzell is representative of singer/song-

Top: *Bob Wills was the father of western swing, a form that built upon traditional fiddle tunes and dance music, but incorporated jazz and swing.*

Above: *Generations – Bill Monroe, Kathy Mattea, Roy Acuff. Acuff, who died in late 1992, was called the "King of Country Music."*

Left: *Bill Monroe and his Bluegrass Boys. Monroe combined several traditional forms to develop the bluegrass sound.*

Left: *Lefty Frizzell's style lives in countless New Country singers. Merle Haggard (above), the most influential of today's stars;* as the Statlers sing, "Half of 'em sound like George [Jones]; half of 'em sound like Merle." Below: *Emmylou Harris.*

writers who followed, carving niches with singing and writing styles; Floyd Tillman, Ernest Tubb, Kitty Wells and others are in this category.

Lefty holds a special place in the timeline because an inordinate number of male singers – those surviving against odds during the pop period, and many today – sing in his style, a back-of-the-throat, crack-voiced, swinging growl-to-croon sound that perfectly fits country lyrics. Merle Haggard is the chief vocal disciple, Johnny Rodriguez and Gene Watson followed, John Anderson sounds like a reincarnation, and Garth Brooks, Joe Diffie and Travis Tritt are in the tradition. When you turn on your car radio these days, half the singers make you think for a moment that you're listening to Lefty or Merle.

Merle is also significant because he, with Willie Nelson and George Jones, form the trio that has maintained the integrity of country music through lean times and high times. They are all conscious of roots and have never compromised their beliefs in, or their devotion to, traditional forms of country music. All have experimented – George with rockabilly, for instance; Willie with pop standards – but they have never left country. That's the difference to their fans, and the difference in their music.

So although these three giants are still active today, and as popular as ever, they are not in this book. They both preceded and transcend New Country. Similarly, the honored artists who held to traditional forms in the period just before the "new traditionalist" explosion are not here, but deserve mention and gratitude. Emmylou Harris came from folk, absorbed rock, and moved to country, where she stays. Hank Williams, Jr. has boogied over to southern rock, but kept the

sounds of his own and his extended family alive through his career. Reba McEntire was a worthy inheritor of Loretta Lynn. All these artists continue as active performers, and popular ones, but this book is devoted to the next generation in these fast-moving times. (Other individual talents should be recognized, too, for keeping their own brand of country flames alive, and for inspiring many of the New Country artists: Johnny Cash, the late Gram Parsons of the Byrds and the Flying Burrito Brothers, Kris Kristofferson.)

And now we're at today. What is the explosion of old sounds that seem new? Why is a new generation hearkening back to its nearly forgotten heritage? What is it about the music that has younger audiences, and urban fans, going wild for what was common to hillbillies 50 years ago? What role do the transfusions of rock and folk and jazz play in New Country's popularity? How can "traditionalism" be "new"? Where are all these overnight success stories coming from – and where are they going?

That is the story of this book, told through the lives of the residents of New Country.

# John Anderson

Right: *A revived career and traditional styles that live in his synthesis with modern forms are hallmarks of John Anderson.*

Bottom: *A country star since the early 1980s, John Anderson has made a strong comeback with his album* Seminole Wind.

There are "forefathers" to the singers in this book, the traditionalists from whom the "new traditionalists" draw inspiration: together they make the story of New Country. But there are also a few names who emerged during the years of country music's wandering in the desert during the 1980s. While George Jones and Merle Haggard and a few others maintained the integrity of country, a few new artists struggled to mold their careers along traditional lines. Truly they, as much as the older legends, paved the way for Randy Travis, Garth Brooks and company. John Anderson was one such singer, and his prescience has served him, for after a decade he is still successfully playing his traditionalist music.

John was born and reared in Florida, and the first music he played was in a rock band. But he soon turned country and absorbed all the influences he could – traditional country, mountain music, southern rock, blues – and all the influences surface in his music today, making John Anderson music hard to classify, except as John Anderson music. His voice is one of Nashville's closest clones of Lefty Frizzell, and he has covered some of Lefty's classics. When he records a rock-flavored song, like "When It Comes to You" (written for him by Mark Knopfler of Dire Straits), John's vocal stylings and his instrumentation make it sound country. His other landmark singles have included "1959," "I'm Just an Old Chunk of Coal," "Your Lyin' Blue Eyes," and his only million-seller to date, "Swingin'."

A testament to John's popularity is his staying power. A 1983 Horizon Award winner from the Country Music Association, he suffered the loss of his label by the end of the decade,

leading many to wonder if his career in country music had peaked. Two years without a record release put a dent in his tour bookings, but after signing with the new BNA label, his recording and radio appeal is as strong as ever. His "comeback" album, *Seminole Wind*, proves that his traditionalist material is as strong and popular as ever, too.

# Clint Black

Left: *Clint Black has been fulfilling the promise of his 1989 CMA Horizon Award since his debut album (*Killin' Time*) went double platinum.*

Randy Travis can be said to be the one who ushered in the "new traditionalist" movement in country music, but Clint Black is probably responsible for what some have called the "hunky-tonk" movement – the first, but not the last, of New Country's male sex symbols. They are good-looking; they highlight their performances with emotional deliveries; and many of them wear western hats. Clint was there early in this genre. He also, following Randy Travis in the "new traditionalist" revival, was the role model for the artist who seemed to come from nowhere, chart immediately with staggering sales numbers, and then share the stage (not quite be eclipsed) with another hat of the same cloth. In this timeline have been Clint, Garth Brooks, Alan Jackson, Billy Ray Cyrus and others.

But none of this is to say that Clint Black (or, for that matter, his successors) is a lightweight performer or a mere flash in the pan. Clint, as archetype, is a substantial and sensitive songwriter, a riveting performer, and a fount of creative versatility. Clint was born in New Jersey, where his father was working as a contract-laborer, but grew up in the Houston area. He was playing and singing by the age of 15, and made his performing debut at the local Benton Springs Club in 1981. For several years he played clubs around Houston while laboring days as an ironworker, until connections took him to Nashville and a recording deal: Hayden Nicholas became a collaborator and co-songwriter; Bill Ham, manager of ZZ Top, signed on as Clint's manager; and Joe Galante of RCA Records Nashville heard demo tapes, saw Clint perform, and signed the promising young musician to a multi-album contract.

Above: *Honky-tonk and rockabilly both live in the music of Clint Black. He is shown here backed by rock 'n' roll pioneer Carl Perkins.*

Right: *Clint was the first New Country singer of the "hat" look.*

Left: The Hard Way *was the title of a Clint Black album – definitely not a description of his meteoric career's progress.*

Above: *Clint Black and his bride, TV actress Lisa Hartman.*

Left: *One of the few things that outnumbers hats in Clint Black's home is music awards.*

It sounds simple, and sounds as if the team headed by Clint knew exactly what success would come with proper management. Indeed the debut album, *Killin' Time*, exploded on country music and crossover charts. Released in May of 1989, it was certified double platinum (two million units sold) less than a year and a half later. An unprecedented five singles from the album became number one hits: "A Better Man," "Killin' Time," "Nobody's Home," "Walking Away" and "Nothing's News." The album retained a number one chart position for 32 consecutive weeks. Clint's second album took less than a year to reach a similar sales plateau, and four singles – the title cut "Put Yourself in My Shoes," "Loving Blind," "One More Payment" and "Where Are You Now" – all broke the Top Five charts. His following album was titled *The Hard Way*. Clint's Country Music Association nomination in 1992 for Vocal Event

of the Year (for the music video *Hold On Partner* with Roy Rogers, whose downturned eyes and boyish smile are presentiments of Clint's appeal) was the latest in a crowded list: CMA Horizon Award (1989) and Top Male vocalist (1990); four 1990 awards from the Academy of Country Music – Album of the Year, Single of the Year, Best New Male Vocalist, and Best Male Vocalist; Nashville Network/Music City News 1990 awards for Star of Tomorrow and Album of the Year.

Recently Clint's off-record activities have had him as much in the spotlight as his songs: he fired manager Bill Ham and filed a $5-million suit against him; Clint in turn was sued by BMG, the German-based owner of RCA, not to leave the label. Some of Clint's clouds were not stormy but silver-lined, however: in late 1991 he married television's glamour girl Lisa Hartman, star of "Knot's Landing."

# Suzy Bogguss

Right: *Suzy's Bogguss's vocals – ranging from plaintive to up-tempo – have marked her as a rising star in New Country.*

Below: *Suzy Bogguss poses with her Academy of Country Music Award in 1992.*

Suzy Bogguss, a beautiful and innovative singer, represents the best aspects of New Country: her voice has the traditional crack and plaintive slides of the great female singers through the years, but her choice of material is pure contemporary. In other words, her sound is New Country, her lyrics are thoughtful, her albums are masterpieces of variety.

Born in Aledo, Illinois, Suzy was reared on folk and country, and toured the Northwest as a singer in the company of her dog Duchess and her cat Chaucer, in a pickup truck and camper. Her first professional break was as a headliner at Dollywood, the Dolly Parton theme park in Tennessee. Landing a recording contract with Capitol Nashville, Suzy gained increasing notice with hits like "Somewhere Between," "Cross My Broken Heart," "Outbound Plane" and "Someday Soon," a countrified version of the Judy Collins love song classic. Also increasing was her mix of introspective material and love songs from a woman's point of view, often penned by herself or other female songwriters, marking a strong position on the landscape of New Country.

Suzy was the recipient of the Academy of Country Music Top New Female Vocalist Award in 1992 and the Horizon Award from the Country Music Association in 1992.

# Garth Brooks

Right: *Garth Brooks has gained phenomenal success with his charismatic performances and the sincerity he conveys with his traditionalist country baritone voice.*

Right: *Garth Brooks's head-mike has become a standard feature of his stage presence.*

Below: *Garth with Sandy Brooks and his parents. Garth's mother, Colleen Carroll, was a 1950s country singer.*

He is a self-proclaimed "chubby kid from Oklahoma," with a degree in advertising after having attended college on a javelin-throwing scholarship, who grew up listening and then performing folk-rock. This kid developed into not just the most representative of New Country artists, but one of the most successful singers in entertainment history. This success, as evidenced by record and ticket sales, not just critical appreciation, coalesced in a remarkable couple of years. The story of Garth Brooks is truly that of a phenomenon.

The youngest son of 1950s country singer Colleen Carroll, performer on TV's "Ozark Jubilee" and Capitol recording artist, Garth only took to music late in his high school years. While attending Oklahoma State he sang in local clubs, gradually mixing country into his repertoire of rock and folk music. In the mid-1980s a tryout at the Opryland Park in Nashville yielded an invitation to join its performance staff, but his

parents urged Garth to complete college studies. The next year, after graduation, he returned to Music City full of cockiness and just about everything else he owned "stuffed into a Honda Accord." In less than a day, after meeting cold shoulders and closed doors instead of his visions of red carpets and fill-in-the-blank contracts, he headed back to Oklahoma. Garth played honky-tonks for several years, paying the dues he naively thought could be skipped. He concentrated on country music, honing his skills and learning to feel the audience.

When he returned to Nashville in 1989, his luck was changed. Garth met Bob Doyle, an ASCAP executive who formed new publishing and management companies, the latter with Pam Lewis, around the singer. Within a few months the team signed a contract with Capitol Records (now Liberty). The label teamed Garth with veteran producer Allen Reynolds, a fortuitous match. Reynolds had shaped the sounds and careers of Crystal Gayle, Don Williams, and most recently Kathy Mattea, and was noted for his trademark soft sounds, gentle arrangements and shuffle beats. But he knew Garth needed a different style, and even recommended a change from his Gary Morris-style vibrato and projection.

Garth reverted to a country baritone: his style became more direct, phrasing in speech patterns rather than musically, and, especially, incorporated a back-of-the-throat crack that conveys emotion and comfortably slides into the Hank Williams/Lefty Frizzell/Merle Haggard tradition.

*Garth Brooks*, the debut album, was released in 1989. Its initial sales were impressive as Garth was being noticed – singles from the album included "If Tomorrow Never Comes," "The Dance," "Not Counting You" and "Much Too Young (To Feel This Damn Old)" – except that the album didn't cool. It kept growing, and to date it has sold nearly five million copies. His next two albums have sold in excess of seven million copies each; *No Fences* contained the rowdy "Friends in Low Places" single, and *Ropin' the Wind* was the only album to knock *No Fences* from a seemingly perpetual spot at the top of album charts – itself a number one album for almost four months. Of course all the country playlists revealed Garth as king of the hill. His videos were also bestsellers, and controversial: portions of *The Thunder Rolls* were banned from country music cable channels for its depiction (by actor Garth Brooks) of domestic violence despite its own censure. Nevertheless the video won a CMA award. An NBC television special built around Garth was one of the top-rated shows of the 1992 season. He guest-starred on the sitcom "Empty Nest," was profiled on network TV's "Dateline," and graced the covers of every type of magazine from supermarket tabloids (no dirt) to investment magazines (marveling at his touch of gold).

His awards are, even for so short a period, hard to enumerate. They include Country Music Association Horizon Award in 1990, CMA Entertainer of the Year in 1991 and 1992, Academy of Country Music Entertainer of the Year Award in 1991 (in fact a total of 10 awards between the two organizations

Above: *Garth's rapport with his audience is a strong element of his appeal. Garth's popularity reached new heights when he become only the second country artist to sing the National Anthem before a Super Bowl, in January 1993.*

Left: *Multi-trophy nights at industry awards ceremonies are getting to be quite common occurrences for Garth Brooks.*

Right: *Garth's head-mike frees him to gyrate, run, dance and even fall into the crowds while he sings at concerts.*

in 1991), Grammies, and fan-voted Nashville Network-Music City News awards. There are also unique accomplishments, such as *Ropin' the Wind* entering the "Billboard" Top-200 album charts at number one, the first time any album has ever done that. Garth is now a member of the Grand Ole Opry.

Perhaps the most remarkable fact, and one that explains Garth's phenomenal popularity, is the personal energy he brings to his music. On record he emits a traditionalist country twang and crack that exults and cries according to the demands of the song, invariably resulting in vocal sincerity. On his videos he conveys power and drama. But his stage shows are

Garth's trademark, fast becoming legendary saturnalias of outrageous stage performance, frenzied audience response, and a good deal of interplay. Garth mugs, flirts and cajoles with the fans. Freed from a mike-stand by a mike-headset, he romps more than Mick Jagger, and he even flies into the sea of fans itself, inevitably caught by a human net while he continues to sing. He laughs, cries (especially about the virtues of home and family), shouts and imparts joy in a total commitment to his craft, his fans and his brand of New Country music, what Garth calls "heart songs." The "heart" attack looks to continue for years to come.

# Brooks and Dunn

Right: *Brooks and Dunn display trophies at the 1992 Academy of Country Music Awards. The duo's music features a hard-edged honky-tonk sound that suits their energetic stage presence.*

Right: *Different personae, different influences, different sounds every time they go out: Kix Brooks and Ronnie Dunn.*

It's not a typical year at the Country Music Association Awards when an act receives a nomination in one category, a win in another, and yet a third triumph – in the "Horizon" category, indicating promise of future success. Brooks and Dunn have promise indeed, but they also have established presence, and success, with their earliest collaborations.

Another interesting fact is that the collaborations of Brooks and Dunn are seasoned, but not old: the pair only met each other in late 1990. They were brought together by Arista Records' head Tim DuBois, who was aware of their abilities separately but had an instinct that as a songwriting and singing team they would click.

Kix Brooks is a Louisiana native who grew up on the street where Johnny Horton and his wife (a former wife of Hank Williams) lived; they provided inspiration and encouragement – "my first exposure to gold records," Kix recalls. It was while in college that he started playing country music regularly – gravitating toward the hard-edged honky-tonk sound that is the trademark of Brooks and Dunn – and eventually spent performing stints in venues as disparate as Alaska (where he also labored on the pipeline), Maine and New Orleans. He wound up as a staff writer with Tree Publishers in Nashville, and composed top hits for top acts: "Bobbie Sue" for the Oak Ridge Boys, "I'm Only In It for the Love" for John Conlee, "Modern Day Romance" for the Nitty Gritty Dirt Band, "Who's Lonely Now" for Highway 101. With Chris Waters, Kix wrote Nashville's official theme song, "I Still Hear the Music."

Ronnie Dunn grew up in Texas loving music; his call became clearer when he was expelled from the Baptist Bible College for playing in local honky-tonks. He moved to Tulsa, associated himself with Leon Russell's entourage, and fronted the house band at the Duke's Country Club. In 1989 Jimmy Oldecker, a friend who is Eric Clapton's drummer, registered Ronnie in the Marlboro Music Talent Roundup competition. Ronnie was unaware until it turned real – and soon he was in Nashville to compete in the national playoffs. He won, and came to the attention of DuBois at Arista.

Brooks and Dunn perform a mix of rock and blues and even Mexican-tinged music, but all under the rubric of country music, honky-tonk style. Their hard-driven stage presence comes across in recordings, but has to be seen to be believed: the laid-back Ronnie remains fairly stationary before the microphone while the animated Kix dances around the entire stage, engaging members of the band and audience alike.

The debut album scored big, and was nominated by the CMA as Album of the Year. "Brand New Man" was the title cut, and a smash single as well. Their follow-up single, "Boot-Scootin' Boogie," was even bigger. Besides their Horizon Award from the CMA in 1992, the newcomers also garnered the Vocal Duo Award, winning out over veterans like the Bellamy Brothers and the Judds. There is little doubt that Brooks and Dunn will be around for a long time.

# Mary-Chapin Carpenter

Right: *Since Mary-Chapin Carpenter's 1989 Academy of Country Music Award for Best New Female Vocalist, she has continued to expand her music horizons, evident in the diversity of her third album,* Shooting Straight in the Dark.

Right: *One of New Country's most circuitous routes has brought Mary-Chapin Carpenter to her successful position.*

Below: *Mary-Chapin's huge audiences invariably contain fans of many backgrounds.*

Mary-Chapin Carpenter is a folksinger who was offered a country music recording contract, a singer with an acoustic guitar fronting a rock 'n' roll band (her description), a certified Yuppie from Princeton, New Jersey, welcomed by hillbilly Nashville, Tennessee.

She grew up in the Ivy League town of Princeton, in Tokyo and in Washington, D.C., listening to folksingers and protest songs. Her first performances were in coffee houses catering to the college crowd. She attended Brown University and graduated with a degree in American Studies, after which she pursued a music career in the Washington area. Her acoustic folk singing won her "Whammy" awards from the Washington Area Music Association, and a demo tape made on the basement equipment of her guitar player impressed Columbia Records, who offered Mary-Chapin a contract in 1987.

It was on her second album, *State of the Heart*, that she found her true musical identity – a bite to her voice and an encompassing range of New Country styles from rock beats to Cajun instrumentation to introspective lyrics. "How Do," a single from the album, yielded her first Top-20 hit, and "This Shirt" placed on Adult Contemporary charts. Her third album,

*Shooting Straight in the Dark*, yielded "Down at the Twist and Shout," an up-tempo Cajun dance tune that had President Bush clapping in time at the 1991 televised Country Music Association Awards. In 1989 the Academy of Country Music named Mary-Chapin Best New Female Vocalist, and in 1992 she won the CMA Best Female Vocalist Award.

# Lionel Cartwright

Below: *After paying his dues in country's "minor leagues," Lionel Cartwright gained multiple successes: as a singer, songwriter, musician and comedian.*

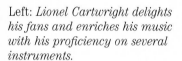

Left: *Lionel Cartwright delights his fans and enriches his music with his proficiency on several instruments.*

Through the years many of country music's superstars have honed their craft on the stages of regional versions of the Grand Ole Opry. A strong presence in the northeastern U.S. continues to be the Wheeling Jamboree in West Virginia. The latest star to "graduate" from the WWVA-based program is Lionel Cartwright.

Lionel was born in Ohio ("only because the hospital was there"), but was reared in West Virginia. A talented singer, songwriter, musician and composer, Lionel was a featured performer on a local radio show while still in high school, moving thereafter to the "Country Cavalcade" on WMNI in Columbus, Ohio. He returned home to Wheeling as a piano player in the house band, the Country Roads, on the Jamboree, working his way up to musical director of the weekly radio concert – while using his earnings to pay for his studies at Wheeling College.

The next step for Lionel was Music City. He was hired by the Nashville Network as star, musical director and arranger on the musical sitcom "I-40 Paradise" and its spinoff "Pickin' at the Paradise." He wrote and performed the theme songs for each show, and was featured in comedy sketches. After television, Lionel concentrated on his singing and songwriting. Signed by MCA, he scored his first Top-20 hit with "Like Father Like Son," a typically homey and faith-tinged song (trademarks of its composers Paul Overstreet and Don Schlitz), and gained national stature with the single "I Watched It All (On My Radio)." The song was an anthem for anyone who grew up a fan of nighttime radio, and Lionel Cartwright's payback to the influences that shaped his promising career.

# Mark Chestnutt

Right: *Mark Chestnutt hit it big with his debut album,* Too Cold at Home, *which featured five number-one songs.*

Below: *Mark Chestnutt – fan of traditional forms and disciple of George Jones.*

Texas and Tennessee have interesting, intertwined histories, going back to the battle of the Alamo, when many Tennesseans (led by Davy Crockett) fought alongside Texans. In later years there has been the combined contribution of western swing – the "western" of country western. Even deeper has been the satellite role that Austin, Texas, has played since the 1970s in being both refuge from and conscience of Music City. Austin singers and songwriters, whether "outlaws" or not, have worked to keep the Nashville Sound honest. Then there are smaller points of contact. Many a singer has not just come from the East Texas and Houston areas, but has been an active performer and a regional recording star before eventually being noticed by Nashville. And many – including Kenny Rogers, Mickey Gilley, Gene Watson, and, now, Mark Chestnutt – have had hits the second time around after their Texas hits have been noticed by Nashville.

So young Mark Chestnutt of Beaumont, Texas, is in good company. He's also in good company in Nashville, as his hero George Jones has taken him under his wing, with advice and a fatherly kind of friendship. He's also in good company among the top breed of the New Country stars, where his records join theirs at the top of record charts.

Mark's real-life father, Bob Chestnutt, was a country music aspirant who played clubs in East Texas and worked for awhile at Music City's Cedarwood Publishing as a songwriter. It was he who turned Mark into a virtual scholar of the branch of country music known as honky-tonk. He played records of Ernest Tubb, Floyd Tillman, George Jones and Merle Haggard for his son; he took him to clubs; he gave his blessing when Mark dropped out of school in the eleventh grade to hit the country music road.

As Mark became a regional star, he recorded a number of modest hits, the biggest of which, "Too Cold at Home," became

Above: *Honky-tonk lives in Mark Chestnutt, maintaining not just the sounds and the words, but the singer's life on the road.*

his first national hit when Mark Wright produced Chestnutt's first album for MCA. Titled after the single, the disc was the biggest debut album in the label's history. Subsequent hits from the new honky-tonker Mark Chestnutt have included "Brother Jukebox," "Your Love Is a Miracle," "Blame It On Texas" and "Broken Promise Land"; his follow-up album was titled *Longnecks and Short Stories*.

# Mark Collie

Left: *New Country star Mark Collie blends honky-tonk, rockabilly and country sounds in his music.*

"My musical roots are like the roots of a tree," says Mark Collie. "They go a long way in every direction." A bright star in the constellation of New Country, he is a little bit honky-tonk, a little bit rockabilly and a lot country, but not a cowboy. In addition, he can write sensitive but raw songs in the tradition of Kris Kristofferson and Willie Nelson, marking him as a notable talent.

Mark grew up in Waynesboro, Tennessee, appropriately midway between Nashville and Memphis, the two musical poles of his personal sound. He got his first job playing in a band at the age of 12. ("I told them I was 14, but I'm sure they didn't believe me. I looked like I was nine.") After high school he played throughout the Southwest, and even in Hawaii for two years, before returning to Tennessee. At one "down" period in Music City, trying to make it as a songwriter, Mark told his wife

Anne he thought he should give up music and get a real (paying) job; she told him if he left music she would leave him. He didn't, she didn't, and now country music fans have a reason to be grateful for that tough-love encouragement.

He was signed by MCA Records and his first two albums, *Hardin County Line* and *Born and Raised in Black and White*, staked his unique position and produced several notable hits. His very first top-charted single, "Something With a Ring To It," was co-written by Aaron Tippin; the song was followed by "Looks Aren't Everything" and "Let Her Go" breaking into the Top Ten.

Besides his musical performances, Mark makes appearances on behalf of diabetes research and care; he has been diagnosed as having the disease, which he monitors carefully on his busy performing schedule.

# Rodney Crowell

Right: *Another New Country star who harkens back to Texas, Rodney Crowell gained critical and commercial success with his 1989 album,* Diamonds and Dirt.

Below right: *Rodney Crowell's stage performances enliven his already electrifying lyrics.*

Right, above and below: *Rodney rose through the ranks as a stage performer, and he instinctively knows how to move his fans. A long wait for recognition has finally yielded fruit with high sales and industry awards.*

Rodney Crowell is one of those New Country luminaries whose star just never seemed to rise high or fast enough for his circle of fans. But, happily, commercial success eventually came. And just as happily, that success has not weakened Rodney's devotion to incisive lyrics and innovation.

He was born and reared in the musical community around Houston, Texas. His grandparents and his father played country music. At first he played rock, but as country allowed more rock and folk influences (especially in experimental Texas), Rodney expanded his horizons. He expanded them geographically when he moved to Nashville in the early 1970s. Jerry Reed was riding a crest at the time, and acquired Rodney's services as a songwriter. The great Texas singer/songwriter Guy Clark introduced Rodney to Emmylou Harris, and he became a member of her Hot Band – fitting in neatly, in that ensemble, with two strains: "new traditionalists" like Ricky Skaggs, who succeeded him; and a folk/rock/country fusion, manifested in Emmylou herself. Rodney was at home in the Hot Band, and penned several of Emmylou's hit songs, including "Amarillo" and "I Ain't Livin' Long Like This." The last song became the title cut of Rodney's first solo album when he signed with Warner in 1977. (Other performers' hits of Rodney's songs include Bob Seger's "Shame on the Moon" and Crystal Gayle's "Till I Gain Control Again.")

Rodney's brand of country, including the hard drive and instrumental improvisation of rock, was evident in his next two albums, which were met with critical raves and modest sales. It was at this time that Rodney met Roseanne Cash, and he became her producer, cowriter, and husband. Their sparkling creativity was the talk of Nashville, and so was their sparring conflict, especially when drugs played a role.

In 1988 Rodney got straight and got a new record contract, with CBS, which provided a new window to his fans. *Street Language* continued as vintage Crowell; the depth, cleverness and sensitivity of his lyrics never ebb. *Diamonds and Dirt*, a 1989 album, was the vehicle in which Rodney finally arrived. Five number one hits, including "It's Such a Small World," "I Couldn't Leave You If I Tried," "She's Crazy For Leavin'" and "After All This Time," which won a Grammy, spun off *Diamonds and Dirt*. The next album was *Keys to the Highway*, which included two haunting tributes to his father, "Many a Long and Lonesome Highway" and "Things I Wish I'd Said," both hits. In 1992 he released *Life Is Messy*, an album animated by the difficulties of his divorce from Roseanne. A smash crossover single, "What Kind of Love," features harmony by Linda Ronstadt and Don Henley; Steve Winwood sings harmony on two other cuts.

The deeper Rodney Crowell explores his life and his moods, the broader his musical horizons become.

29

# Billy Ray Cyrus

Left: *As talented a songwriter as he is a performer, Billy Ray Cyrus penned six of the 10 songs on his debut album,* Some Gave All.

Right: *The source of the epidemic sweeping America known as the "Cyrus Virus," Billy Ray Cyrus has attracted a younger, wider audience to New Country.*

In late 1992 the "Cyrus Virus" hit the United States of America. Billy Ray Cyrus seemed to come out of nowhere, captivating country music fans with his electrifying performances. His first records were being played on country music stations, on rock stations, on short-wave radio. His veterans' anthem, "Some Gave All," was named as the official tune of the Vietnam observance rally on Veteran's Day in Washington, D.C., and was played simultaneously on virtually every country station in America. He was interviewed on "Good Morning America" and has been pictured on the covers of magazines and newspapers across the country.

It was as if the impetus toward large-scale acceptance of New Country took a quantum leap beyond levels thought un-attainable, breaking records thought untouchable, all because of the Cyrus Virus. Billy Ray, a country rocker but pure country, has confirmed the massive new acceptance of country music across America, by attracting a wider, younger – and larger – audience.

He is also a phenomenon in other ways. Billy Ray is the latest "hunky-tonk hero" or "country hunk," but he doesn't wear a hat. In fact there are other pieces of clothing he doesn't wear either, progressing through his stage act; he might be the first of what could be called "Chippendale Country." And in the style of some rock idols, he sings, plays and gyrates amidst the tossed lingerie of female fans in the invariably screaming, swaying audiences.

Billy Ray grew up in Flatwoods, Kentucky, the grandson of a preacher and the son of a gospel-band musician. His first dream was to be big-league baseball player, not a singer, but when he fixed on the idea of performing music he formed a band, Sly Dog, and began touring. He gravitated toward outlaw country and southern rock. When a fire destroyed his band's equipment, Billy Ray took it as a sign, he says; he moved to Los Angeles, formed a new band and performed locally while selling cars by day in Woodland Hills. In 1986 he moved back to Kentucky, his base for headlining during the week at the Ragtime Lounge in Huntington, West Virginia, and traveled most weekends to Nashville to pitch his material. So went the first 10 years of Billy Ray's career in music.

The next year Grand Ole Opry star Del Reeves heard a Billy Ray tape, recorded one of his songs, and recommended him to veteran manager Jack McFadden, whose former clients included Buck Owens and Merle Haggard. Soon Mercury Records personnel caught Billy Ray's electrifying live performances and signed him to a contract. (In late 1992 Reeves sued Billy Ray, claiming that he had been promised special compensation from "the son I never had" if Billy Ray ever became a major success.) Six of the 10 songs on Billy Ray's debut album, *Some Gave All*, were written by himself; on one, he shares credit and royalties with an ex-roommate who threw him out and uttered lines of unconscious inspiration. The biggest splash of all, though, came with "Achy Breaky Heart," a song written by Don Von Tress.

Above: *Billy Ray's evocative performances – the sexiest since Elvis's – heat him up. And they seem to have the same effect on his female fans, many of whom toss lingerie on stage at his feet.*

Right: *In tails and denim jeans, the unconventional Billy Ray poses at the 1992 Billboard Music Awards.*

Mercury helped the song by using classic merchandising moves. Instead of releasing the videos in advance of the radio cuts, promotions were sent to country music dance clubs across the nation. A multilevel program was offered: free materials including cassettes to the clubs; a video of Billy Ray performing "Achy Breaky Heart" with an instructional dance segment; an invitation to hold dance contests, with winners to be flown to Nashville for TV appearances; and the winning club to receive a complimentary concert appearance by Billy Ray. After the buildup, *then* the music videos and radio station cuts were released. How much was the promotion responsible for the success of "Achy Breaky Heart"? No one could tell amidst the frenzy of the Cyrus Virus. While millions danced the Achy Breaky, Billy Ray was awarded Single of the Year honors at the Country Music Association ceremonies in 1992. It promises to be the first of many honors for the preacher's grandson with a rockin' guitar and dancin' shoes. Billy Ray sang the National Anthem before the first game of the 1992 World Series – the pairing of two national pastimes of the moment.

# Billy Dean

Right: *Billy Dean has become known for his introspective lyrics, but is as personable as anyone in New Country.*

Below: *Garnering trophies at the 1992 Academy of Country Music Awards, Billy Dean (with Celia Froelig) basks in the glory of making it big after a decade in Music City.*

Billy Dean moved to Nashville from his native Florida in the early eighties. Reared on country music, he was the regional winner in the Wrangler Starsearch Contest, and placed among the finalists in the national playoffs in Nashville. Billy remained in Music City and formed a band that opened for Mel Tillis, Ronnie Milsap, Steve Wariner and others.

A performer since his teens, Billy also has been a natural songwriter, so during his days of touring out of Nashville his compositions were recorded by many artists, including Milsap, Randy Travis and Shelly West. It was publisher/producer Jimmy Gilmer who noticed Billy and arranged a BMI composers' contract, and then a recording deal with SBK Records. The big break came when Billy appeared in the New Faces Show at the 1991 Country Radio Seminar in Nashville. His performance of "Only Here For a Little While" caught the attention of the assembled music directors and programmers, and Billy's career as a major star was assured when the song was released as a single.

The breakthrough hit was followed by the single "Somewhere in My Broken Heart," which has become Billy's signature song. The hit was a number one, and represents his best singing/songwriting mode, that of tender introspection.

In 1991 Billy Dean was a finalist in the Country Music Association's Horizon Award category. Indeed Billy has been all over Nashville's horizon, and – with his appealing style – will be there for some time to come.

# Diamond Rio

They are six musicians and singers who were originally called the Tennessee River Boys. They took their new name from the 18-wheeler that dominates America's highways, and though they later realized that the truck was spelled "Reo," they kept their spelling because it seemed, well, southwestern, or contemporary or different. Different. That describes the background, the members and the music of Diamond Rio.

Tim DuBois of Arista Records signed the group after he heard them open a show for George Jones in Alabama. A single from their debut album, "Meet in the Middle," became a number one hit – the first time in country music history that a vocal group's debut single achieved that rank. Their follow-up single also broke into the Top Five.

Above: *A group with hybrid influences but a unified sound – Diamond Rio.*

The band features an eclectic mixture of rock beats, blue-grass harmonies, solid country themes, and, sometimes, even jazz instrumentation. Marty Roe (whose first performance was singing Merle Haggard's "I'm a Lonesome Fugitive" at the age of three) sings lead vocals. Dana Williams, bass and vocals, is nephew to bluegrass legends Sonny and Bob (the Osborne Brothers), and has been part of the road shows of Vassar Clements and Jimmy C. Newman. Jimmy Olander, who taught banjo playing to others when he was 12 and who has performed with Duane Eddy and Rodney Crowell, masters a Telecaster

Bottom: *Respect and acceptance have come quickly to Diamond Rio, evidenced by their 1991 Academy of Country Music Award for Vocal Group of the Year.*

Right: *The six musicians who comprise the group Diamond Rio are some of the most respected talents in New Country. There is safety – and excitement – in numbers, as the members mix it up in live performances.*

hybrid known as a Taxicaster as Diamond Rio's lead guitar. Gene Johnson, who has been a sideman with David Bromberg and J.D. Crowe & the New South, plays mandolin and fiddle. Pianist Dan Truman is classically trained and brings yet another wrinkle to the group's sound, and Brian Prout, drums, is married to Wild Rose's drummer Nancy Given.

Diamond Rio was nominated as Vocal Group of the Year by the Country Music Association in 1991, and won the award in 1992; they also won the same category award from the Academy of Country Music in 1991.

# Joe Diffie

Right: *Joe Diffie, described by many in Nashville as having "a perfect country voice," topped the charts with his debut album* A Thousand Winding Roads.

Below: *When New Country artists hearken back to the old traditions, there is no deeper wellspring than Jimmie Rodgers. Joe Diffie captured his sound and style in his hit "Startin' Over Blues."*

Joe Diffie's style incorporates no-nonsense, straight-ahead, emotional, crack-in-the-voice, freewheeling, traditionalist country vocals – the essence of New Country. His debut single, "Home," indicates just where he is comfortable in the country tradition: in the country tradition.

He came to it slowly, although not, as with some other New Country artists, because of infatuations with other forms of music. Growing up in Oklahoma, Joe wanted to be a doctor, and worked in a foundry until he could study. But he got the "music bug," and when his factory closed and his marriage failed, he moved to Nashville to give the bug some room. It was 1986. He got another factory job, this time with Gibson Guitars, while on evenings and weekends he wrote songs and eventually entered the field of demo-singing.

Epic Records signed Joe, believing in his pure country voice and that his commitment to traditionalist material spelled success. They were proved correct, as Joe's debut album *A Thousand Winding Roads* shot to the top of the charts, and the single "Home" became the label's first number one hit by a debut artist. More impressively, three other singles from the album were also number one hits: "If You Want Me To," "If the Devil Danced in Empty Pockets," and "New Way to Light Up an Old Flame." His second album was entitled *Regular Joe* and premiered amidst similar raves.

Joe has been nominated as Top New Male vocalist by the Academy of Country Music and Male Vocalist of the Year by the Country Music Association.

# Holly Dunn

Right: *Holly Dunn writes and performs songs that range from sensitive introspection to hard-driven rockers.*

Below: *Holly Dunn communicates songs of home and heart in a genuine manner, comfortable with who she is and what she has to say.*

A preacher's daughter, an aspiring songwriter from Texas, a talented singer with good looks ... the type is actually common in country music. But Holly Dunn does not really fit many stereotypical molds. Certainly her family and background contributed to her rise, and their influence still is a part of her success; Holly's breakthrough single, "Daddy's Hands," (1986) was written about her dad, and her brother Chris Waters is her producer-songwriting partner.

In college Holly sold a hit song to gospel singer Christy Lane. Then in Nashville she worked a desk-job at a music publishing house while writing songs that eventually were recorded by Louise Mandrell, the Whites, and Terri Gibbs.

Finally, in the mid-1980s, Holly was signed as a singer with MTM Records which, before it went out of business, charted several of her songs and albums, including "Daddy's Hands." On the strength of that warm, sentimental classic she won the Country Music Association's Horizon Award in 1987. She was picked up by Warner Bros., and accumulated Grammy nominations and country music industry awards.

Holly Dunn covers an impressive range in her choice of material, which well suit her vocal stylings: in introspective songs she is breathy and sensitive, but she can also belt out hard-driven up-tempo rockers. Perhaps the most striking aspect of her work is integrity. A promising single, "Maybe I Mean Yes," was being misconstrued by some to encourage date rape, and Holly pulled the song from circulation. It is through songwriting and singing that Holly Dunn communicates, and she does it as well as anyone in the New Country.

# Vince Gill

Right: *After honing his performing and songwriting skills for a decade, Vince Gill gained widespread success and industry awards in the 1990s.*

Below: *Quiet Vince Gill has been in the spotlight for years, but only recently has a large audience noticed.*

In a way, it seems like Vince Gill has been around forever, the Ronald Reagan of country music (referring to Reagan's film roles as the nice guy who never got the girl). If there were an award for the artist receiving most predictions of stardom, Vince would have swept the ceremonies. On the other hand, it seems surprising that it's a decade since he did chart with occasional hit singles, and won an Academy of Country Music New Male Vocalist award (1984). It just seemed that Vince Gill would be a perennial Secret Weapon, a walking piece of Inside Information.

That is, until he hit with the album *When I Call Your Name.* He was with a new label, MCA, although the material he produced on three previous RCA albums was little different. He was working with old friends among the musicians and producers, but that was not different, either. Perhaps things just caught up with Vince Gill who, in his laid-back and amiable way, as one of the most popular artists in Music City, has merely exercised integrity and commitment to quality in his patient climb to the top of his profession.

A "new traditionalist"? Vince Gill's records are mainstream country in subject matter and instrumentation, yet something makes his listeners discern bluegrass in his roots. In fact Vince has impeccable credentials in bluegrass music, but only subtly do those strains come through today. Rather it is the essence (instead of instrumentation) of bluegrass that he conveys, singing in a beautiful, mournful, soulful, arresting counter-tenor voice. Bill Monroe has it, and so have others, but the important factor is not the register but the emotion. Vince can take possession of an audience, reducing a crowd to rapt silence when he sings his lonesome hurt songs or heartfelt love songs.

Vince grew up in Oklahoma, where his father (now an appellate judge) played banjo in a local pickup band; young Vince listened to bluegrass and formed the Mountain Smoke Band. After high school he moved to Kentucky and joined the Bluegrass Alliance (with luminaries Sam Bush and Dan Crary), played briefly with Ricky Skaggs in Boone Creek, and then moved to California to play for two years with Byron Berline's Sundance progressive bluegrass group. He was then invited to join Pure Prairie League, where his inspired instrumentals, lead vocals and clever songwriting moved him to the forefront. The group with Vince fronting had two Top Ten hits, and he started to attract attention.

When he married Janis Oliver (half of the excellent Sweethearts of the Rodeo duet team) Vince switched groups once again to Rodney Crowell's back-up band, the Cherry Bombs. Rodney might be the runner-up in Nashville's long-predicted-success sweepstakes with Vince, but his band at the time (including such future Vince Gill collaborators – as producers – Emory Gordy, Jr. and Tony Brown) was notable for its quality and versatility.

Capping Vince's rise was his work as studio musician in Nashville. He has sung harmony and played amazing guitar riffs on hundreds of albums, so the Music City community gradually became unofficial members of the Vince Gill fan club through watching him sing and play. His MCA debut album featured a song co-written by Roseanne Cash, a duet with Reba McEntire, and the smash title song, "When I Call Your Name," whose haunting background vocals were provided by Patty Loveless (with whom he subsequently recorded a duet album). As his material regularly began to be certified gold ($1 million in sales) and platinum (a million units sold), Vince picked up industry awards: 1990 and 1992 Country Music Association Song of the Year ("When I Call Your Name" and "Look At Us," respectively); 1991 and 1992 Country Music Association Male Vocalist of the Year; 1991 Music City News Instrumentalist of the Year; CMA nomination as Entertainer of the Year (1992); and so forth, including Grammies. The new member of the Grand Ole Opry was co-host of the televised CMA Awards (with Reba McEntire) in 1992. Considering Vince's deliberate rise to the top, he is one artist about whom all who "knew him when" can say they were correct in predicting his stardom; it was just indeed a question of time.

Left: *A trio of great singers and killer pickers – (left to right) Steve Warriner, Ricky Skaggs and Vince Gill – at the Grammy Awards.*

Above and right: *Vince combines the haunting high tenor of traditional mountain music with modern sensibilities.*

# Alan Jackson

Right: *The 1991 Top New Male Artist of the Year (ACM) and 1992 Male Vocalist of the Year (CMA), Alan Jackson worked his way up in Nashville from mailroom clerk to New Country superstar.*

Below and right: *Lanky Alan Jackson strides onto a stage, modestly tips his hat to the applause, quietly goes into his act – and masterfully captures the audience.*

"You know that country song 'Who's Gonna Fill Their Shoes'? I don't know whether I can fill 'em, but I'd sure like to try 'em on."

The speaker is Alan Jackson, and he refers to the George Jones hit song. In identifying with the likes of the legendary "Possum," Jackson demonstrates why he is one of the most representative of the New Country stars. Further, he displays that taste, not tradition, puts him in the ranks of the "new traditionalists". Alan never was a rabid fan of, nor seriously thought about performing, country music until he was in his twenties.

But at that time the native of Newnan, Georgia, was affected by two circumstances. A friend started to fly small planes with an eye toward gaining a commercial airline license, and he did it, inspiring Alan to set a goal and pursue it. Then, after he considered moving to Nashville to try his hand at music, his wife Denise met Glen Campbell in an airport. She spoke of her husband's goal and he gave her the business card of his publishing company in Music City.

Right: *With a jukebox motif on his stage set (inspired by his hit "Don't Rock the Jukebox"), Alan Jackson has been rocking jukeboxes since he hit the New Country scene with his quality music and trademark white hat.*

Below: *Success has not spoiled the unpretentious Alan Jackson. Featuring number one singles "Wanted," "Chasin' That Neon Rainbow," and "I'd Love You All Over Again," his debut album* Here in the Real World *went platinum in a year.*

Success is not automatic, however, especially in country music stories. Alan's first job was in the mailroom at the Nashville Network, and on the side he wrote songs, performed locally, and made contacts – for instance, with Randy Travis, who at the time was a cook and singer at a Nashville club. Alan went on staff as songwriter for Campbell's publishing company before rejoining Travis, who was by this time a star, as his opening act on tour. The tall, quiet gentleman with long blond hair and blue eyes, whose songs invariably reflect sentimental love and solid virtue, fell in with the wave of New Country singers wearing trademark hats (Alan's is white).

His first album, *Here in the Real World*, March 1990, went platinum, and the spinoff video, *Here in the Reel World*, went gold. His second album spun off a succession of single hits, including the smash title song "Don't Rock the Jukebox." There is a reference in the song to George Jones, and the album in-cludes a tribute to his mentor, "Just Playin' Possum." Another tribute song is the haunting tale about Hank Williams, "Midnight in Montgomery." The album went platinum in six months. Alan has garnered many industry nominations for singing and songwriting, including Male Vocalist of the Year and Entertainer of the Year from the Country Music Association (1992), and among his wins are the Academy of Country Music's Top New Male Artist of the Year (1991) and CMA's Best Music Video (1992) for *Midnight in Montgomery*.

The unpretentious Alan Jackson and his friend Randy Travis continue to cowrite songs for each other's albums, and Alan's friendship with George Jones is reflected by fan-oriented bumper stickers they each sport for the other on their pickup trucks. Putting his sudden stardom in perspective, Alan comments, "I found myself thinking: 'Here I am on *Hee Haw*, in the corn field. I guess I really have made it!'"

# Hal Ketchum

Right: *Hal Ketchum grew up in the small town of Greenwich, New York, in the Adirondacks. He spent more than a decade as a carpenter. Hal brings this background to bear in his music: his finely-crafted songs focus on small towns, common folks and everyday concerns.*

Below: *In songs like "My Daddy's Oldsmobile," Hal Ketchum brings to New Country the storytelling tradition of the singer/songwriter.*

You might say singer/songwriter Hal Ketchum is a square peg in a round hole. He entered the country music scene late, spending most of his 40-something years as a carpenter; he hails from New York State, not exactly a seedbed of national country stars; his first album was released in Germany; he is vocal about his leftish politics, which are definitely against the grain of the Nashville norm. But despite these differences there are solid reasons – beyond the quality material and sincere vocal stylings – for Hal's success as a New Country star.

In 1981 Hal moved to Gruene, Texas, an active folk-country-rock center of the Austin Sound. Hal became a regular at Gruene Hall, first as fan, then as performer, all the while absorbing themes and styles. He abandoned carpentry as his main activity once singing and songwriting were in his blood, and moved to Nashville in 1990.

Hal was signed by Forerunner Music and assigned to producer Allen Reynolds, who has through the years helped mold the sounds and careers of Crystal Gayle, Garth Brooks and Kathy Mattea. With Reynolds co-producing, Ketchum's first album, for Curb, was *Past the Point of Rescue*, with Mattea singing harmony on some cuts. "Small Town Saturday Night" was a smash hit single, the biggest country music radio song of 1991, according to a trade journal. "Small Town" is representative of

Hal's subsequent offerings and his thematic preoccupations; it mirrors Hal's concerns with small towns, common folks and blue heartaches.

Hal's voice displays the same versatility as his choice of material. He growls smoothly and shouts excitedly; he can be desultory or intense. "I Know Where Love Lives" is an introspective ballad (and his second major hit); "Five O'Clock World" is a cover of the 1960s hit from Jay and the Americans, written, incidentally, by Hal's producer Allen Reynolds.

# Tracy Lawrence

Below: *Tracy Lawrence – seen here performing on Jerry Jeff Walker's "Texas Connection" TV show – found early acceptance as his releases shot to number one spots on music charts.*

Left: *With his clear, new traditionalist voice and his appealing songs, Tracy Lawrence has made his mark in Nashville and beyond.*

Tracy Lawrence is a New Country star whose determination to make his mark on country music couldn't be stopped by the proverbial bullets – and not the kind on the *Billboard* charts, either. He was mugged on the streets of Nashville just after cutting his album *Sticks and Stones*, and took four bullets that injured his hip, arm and knee. Three months of recovery and therapy saw him back on the road. "Performing is all I think about right now," said the tall singer who is in his mid-twenties, referring even to marriage: "I'm long way from settling down."

Born in Texas and reared in Arkansas, Tracy spent his college years in equal parts of studying, carousing and playing music. One day he decided to get serious about his music, and moved to Nashville. He remembers the experience: "It was September 2, 1990, a Monday night, and it was nine o'clock. I hit that I-295 bypass and saw that Nashville skyline . . . and felt like I was home." He made himself at home quickly, and had breaks that brought him a recording contract in less than a year, and two quick number one hits – "Sticks and Stones" and "Today's Lonely Fool" – in less than another year. His clear, new traditionalist voice, his choice of quality songs to record, and his determination will keep Tracy Lawrence before his growing number of fans for a long time.

# Patty Loveless

Left: *With her rich and supple voice, Patty Loveless breathes life into her songs, which range from honky-tonk and blues to balladry.*

Y ou know that the "new traditionalism" has arresting appeal, and an artist is a committed member of the New Country scene, when things come together this way: a promising country vocalist leaves the field and moves away from Nashville at the time of the pop invasion; she becomes a regional rock act and doesn't even hear about the changes in country music; when she is introduced to the new wave of New Country, she returns to Nashville, returns to performing, and returns to country music in a big way. Patty Loveless followed such a path, and is now a premiere leader of the "new traditionalist" sound.

As indicated, Patty has actually had three careers. She was born Patty Ramey in Pikeville, Kentucky, a coal miner's daughter. Her family moved to Louisville when Patty was 10 so her father could receive medical attention for a work-related condition. She grew up listening mostly to mountain and bluegrass music, but started performing at 12 with her brother, Roger, at local shows. At 14 she visited Nashville and met Porter Wagoner, from whose office she was introduced around Music Row, and whose singing partner Dolly Parton befriended her. Patty crossed paths with another great female talent in country

music at the time, Kentucky cousin Loretta Lynn. The Wilburn Brothers were losing Loretta as an opening act, and offered Patty the chance to sing, travel and write for their publishing house Sure Fire (but not to record). Except for time taken to finish high school in Louisville, Patty spent the next few years writing songs and doing local touring with the Wilburns.

Then Patty ran away with the Wilburns' drummer Terry Lovelace to North Carolina, where for 10 years she sang in clubs and honky-tonks, and sang mostly rock. She dealt with a repertoire she seldom now calls upon, but she did develop a drive to her style and an edge to her voice that currently serve her well.

In 1985 her brother urged her to return to Nashville. Some folks remembered her – even though she was now Patty Loveless (a variation on her recently divorced husband's name) – and she signed a deal with MCA Records. Her amazing command of honky-tonk, ballads and blues – like in the achy, remarkable "Can't Stop Myself From Loving You" – is solidly based on country music, defining, today, what "new traditionalism" is all about. Produced by Emory Gordy, Jr. (whom she ultimately married), Patty has progressively scored with Top 40, Top Ten and number one albums and singles since her self-titled debut album and its first hit "After All." She has won industry awards, joined the Grand Ole Opry, toured with Clint Black, George Strait and Hank Williams, Jr., and sung memorable duets with Vince Gill.

Above left: *Patty Loveless has gone through several evolutions – career segments, musical styles, even professional names – and has settled into a comfortable and winning sound in New Country.*

Left: *Patty Loveless won the American Music Award for Best New Country Artist.*

Right: *Patty sings "Can't Stop Myself from Loving You." One of the best solo acts in New Country, Patty is also in demand as a duet partner, most recently with Marty Stuart.*

# Kathy Mattea

Right: *New Country star Kathy Mattea has worked her way up in Nashville, from tour guide at the Country Music Hall of Fame to recording artist. Her hit song "Eighteen Wheels and a Dozen Roses" put her at the top of sales charts longer than any other female singer in a decade.*

Right: *Kathy Mattea is living proof that traditional country modes can mix with influences from other styles like folk music and Irish fiddle tunes, as she tours with a variety of guest musicians.*

Oftentimes singers experiment with different styles and influences during their climb upward in the music business; and when success arrives they just as often firmly settle into a style with which they became identified. To some, this style is an affirmation of what got them to where they are. To others, what they really settle into is a rut.

But to Kathy Mattea it is the other way around. The singer/songwriter from Cross Lanes, West Virginia, has broadened her musical horizons and experimented with new sounds throughout the stages of her increasingly successful career. She's still country – one of the most prominent of the New Country stars, in fact – but invites influences of folk, blues and story songs into her style.

It was folk music that first attracted Kathy, and first compelled her to pick up acoustic guitars. Her first group, while she was a student at West Virginia University, was a folk group. She followed a member of that group to Nashville in the late 1970s

and when he returned to West Virginia, Kathy stayed in Music City. One of her first jobs was as a tour guide at the Country Music Hall of Fame, playing hostess to many visitors who would no doubt later be her fans. She had other jobs, too, as a waitress and a compositor, and as a singer on demo tapes that songwriters would send to record companies or big-name singers. She also was the center of a group of aspiring singers and songwriters, hosting potluck dinners at her apartment. All these contacts brought her into the limelight, first as a performer at local clubs, then to a contract with Polygram Records. As her recording identity evolved from a pop flavor to individualized and experimental themes, vocal styles and arrangements, producer Allen Reynolds – who has guided many recording careers from Don Williams to Garth Brooks – oversaw Kathy's emergence. Her throaty alto was developed, and her material became less lavishly produced. Her songs strayed from standard country lyrics to introspection and reflective story songs.

Left: *When singer/songwriters meld several traditions into the "new traditionalism," country music doesn't lose, it gains – and so do fans of New Country talents like Kathy Mattea.*

Right: *Kathy Mattea won the Academy of Country Music's Female Vocalist of the Year Award – one of the many honors she has gained for her talent and innovation.*

Below: *Kathy and her husband Jon Vezner, who with Don Henry wrote "Where've You Been," a remarkable story-song hit for Kathy. Although the couple had faith in the song, it was appended to an album without the thought that it would impress listeners in New Country and in crossover markets.*

Her first Top Ten hit was "Love at the Five and Dime"; her first number one hit as "Goin' Gone." Songs that followed include "Times Passes By," "Eighteen Wheels and a Dozen Roses" – which put her at the top of sales charts longer than any other female country singer in a decade – and the amazing story-song cowritten by her husband Jon Vezner and Don Henry, "Where've You Been." The song is a tender, sparse, personal tale of a couple having reached old age, of their reflections and, because of failing memories, about lost reflections. Delivered with soulful simplicity, Kathy's song attracted attention and affection, sweeping award ceremonies and garnering crossover attraction.

Among the other awards in Kathy's short career have been Female Vocalist of the Year from the Country Music Association (1989 and '90) and the Academy of Country Music (1990); and Single Record of the Year from the CMA and ACM in 1988. *Time Passes By*, an album that featured a hit of its title song, was a collection of songs that were more personal favorites than sure-fire commercial hits. The choices proved to be both personal and commercial, confirming the wisdom of Kathy's individualist direction.

# Lorrie Morgan

Right: *Lorrie Morgan became the youngest member of the Grand Ole Opry in 1984. Six years later her debut album,* Leave the Light On, *went gold, confirming country fans' enthusiasm for Lorrie's vocal versatility.*

Right: *No longer is Lorrie Morgan dismissed as "George Morgan's little girl."*

Perseverance and overcoming – those have been the hallmarks of Lorrie Morgan's rise to the top of New Country singers. She has had to overcome some unusual obstacles. For one, her father, George Morgan, was a popular country singer ("Candy Kisses," "Room Full of Roses"; duet singer with Marion Worth and Rosemary Clooney; member of the Grand Ole Opry), and while there were plusses to having a famous father, Lorrie had to contend with being dismissed as merely her father's daughter. Similarly, her looks are a two-edged sword. Her stunning platinum blonde hair and lounge-singer attire cannot hurt

a performer, except when someone like Lorrie Morgan is dismissed as a mere pretty face.

But Lorrie Morgan has paid her dues. She sang on the Ryman Auditorium's Grand Ole Opry stage when she was 13; later opened and sang back-up with George Jones on tour; was named to the Grand Ole Opry herself in 1984; and was on the staff of the "Nashville Now" television show. No one is dismissing Lorrie or her talent any more. And despite her nightclub dresses, she sings straight country . . . even less pop-oriented than her father's music.

If there is an overriding thematic preoccupation in Lorrie's music, it is that of the sad side of love. Among the trage-dies in her life was the unexpected death in 1989 of her hus-band Keith Whitley, who was surely one of the New Country's brightest talents and the father of Lorrie's baby boy, Jesse. There is a melancholy aspect to much of Lorrie's music that is not a trademark (like, for instance, her father's "rose" songs) but rather a foundation of depth and sensitivity. Her first albums (for RCA) were certified gold and spun off a succession of number one single hits. In 1990, while touring with Clint Black, Lorrie fell in love with Clint's driver, Brad Thompson. The pair was married the following year.

Above and right: *Lorrie Morgan's dynamic and emotional performances endear her to millions of New Country fans.*

Left: *Lorrie with her late husband Keith Whitley, who had travelled a path similar to Ricky Skaggs's and Marty Stuart's, from bluegrass to New Country.*

# Lee Roy Parnell

Right: *Lee Roy Parnell's Texas brand of country – synthesizing elements of blues, folk, jazz, gospel and swing – embodies the new traditionalism.*

Below: *Lee Roy Parnell returning home, performing before a Texas audience on TV's "Austin City Limits."*

A lot of Texans are in the center of the New Country movement, and there is a good reason. The influences that have made up the Texas brand of country music through the years – country, gospel, blues, swing, jazz, folk – are also ingredients in the new mixture of traditionalist sounds that comprise New Country. Lee Roy Parnell is the very embodiment of those diverse but compatible strains.

Lee Roy was raised on a ranch outside Abilene. Western swing legend Bob Wills, at the end of his career, was a family friend who visited the ranch and invited the six-year-old Lee Roy to sing on his radio show. In 1987 Lee Roy moved to Nashville as a songwriter for Welk Music, and two years later recorded an album for Arista that won high critical praise.

In his second album, in 1992, Lee Roy settled more comfortably into his own musical identity. He simplified the arrangements, starting each recording session with just his guitar and vocals, but seldom building more than another guitar, bass, drums, and occasionally a piano. The title song, "Love Without Mercy," written by the talented Mike Reid and Don Pfrimmer, set the tone for the album with its gentle soulfulness and introspection; but the collection is built around the spinoff single "The Rock," a traditional country-style song with gospel undertones. Lee Roy Parnell is happy to be a crucible, inheriting and mixing the diverse influences of his background, and forming them into something a little old and little new, but always somehow fresh.

# Collin Raye

Right: *After many years playing on the road in clubs, Collin Raye hit it big with his debut album* All I Can Be.

Below: *Collin Raye – young but veteran, country but fusion.*

Although in his early thirties, Collin Raye has been singing and performing for more than half of his life. It's in the blood. His mother, Lois, was a regional act in Arkansas and Texas and once opened on a flatbed-truck show for Elvis, Jerry Lee Lewis, Johnny Cash and Carl Perkins. Collin was born Floyd Wray in DeQueen, Arkansas, was reared in Texarkana, and eventually formed a band with his brother, Scott, and became a regional act of note in the Northwest and in Reno clubs.

The Wray Brothers recorded briefly for Mercury, but when Collin Raye, as a single act, attracted the attention of producer Jerry Fuller, a contract with Epic resulted. The title song of his debut album, "All I Can Be," was a surprise hit, highlighted by harmony by Vince Gill (a counterpoint to Raye's own distinctive vocals, which range from leathery low ranges to sweet tenor, almost in Vince's own registers). The next hit off the album was "Love, Me," a hauntingly beautiful love song that was nominated by the Country Music Association in 1992 as Song of the Year. His follow-up was another sensitive love song, "In This Life." Teaming with Collin on his smash debut album were quality sidemen like Herb Pederson and Jay Dee Maness of the Desert Rose Band, Fred Tackett of Little Feat, steel player Paul Franklin of Dire Straits and others who distinguish Collin Raye by the company he keeps.

59

# Ricky Van Shelton

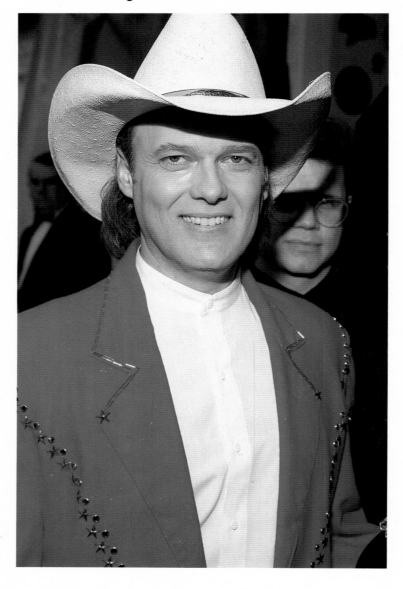

Right: *With his smooth baritone voice and his traditional sound, Ricky Van Shelton brings country music back to its roots.*

Right: *Ricky Van Shelton personifies Grit – the name of his hometown in Virginia, and the character trait he displays in pursuing his goals in music.*

Most New Country stars certify their status as "new traditionalists" by hearkening back to the sounds of the proud country music heritage. Ricky Van Shelton is one who planted his roots by a number of "covers" (updated versions) of classic country tunes. His early albums, and hit singles, were peppered with remakes of such favorites as "Life Turned Her That Way," "Statue of a Fool," "From a Jack to a King," and "Life's Little Ups and Downs." It's called going to the source.

Ricky's other source is home – Grit, Virginia, where he was reared, working as a pipe fitter and listening to The Beatles and The Rolling Stones, not country music. His brother once asked Ricky to drive him and his music-making friends to a bluegrass jam, and the only way Ricky would drive, he remembers, was if he could get behind the wheel of the Ford Fairlane 289. He did, but it wasn't the biggest thrill of the evening: Ricky took to country music that night, and hasn't stopped driving

*that* classic since. Eventually he and his wife Bettye moved to Nashville where he began the tried-and-true routine of working day jobs, looking for performance gigs, cutting demo tapes and making contacts.

A tape made its way to CBS Records and Ricky was soon signed to a contract, soon recorded an album, and soon was one of the top singers in country music. The album, *Wild Eyed Dream*, was quickly certified platinum, selling a million units. Subsequent albums (*Loving Proof*, *RVS III*, *Backroads*, a great gospel album *Don't Overlook Salvation* and *Greatest Hits Plus*) and top-charted singles (including "Don't We All Have the Right," "I Meant Every Word He Said," and "I'll Leave This World Loving You") by the handsome, reserved, smooth-voiced baritone have cemented Ricky's style and popularity. An acting career may be in his future; his video with Dolly Parton based on the duet "Rockin' Years" has been one of the best-received of

Left: *Ricky Van Shelton with Kathy Mattea. Awards and recognitions have been plentiful for both stars of New Country.*

Above: *For all his success, Ricky Van considers his fans one of his most important assets. And his fans love him dearly.*

the form. Among Ricky's many awards have been Top New Male Vocalist from the Academy of Country Music (1987), Horizon Award from the Country Music Association (1988, the same year he became a member of the Grand Ole Opry), Star of Tomorrow from Music City News (1988), Favorite Newcomer from the Nashville Network (1988); Best Male Vocalist from the CMA (1989); and Entertainer of the Year from the fan-voted Nashville Network-Music City News Awards in 1990 and '91. With his appealing voice, the diversity of his music styles, his unpretentious manner and his dedication to New Country, Ricky Van will continue to occupy a special place in the hearts of his many fans.

# Ricky Skaggs

Left: *Ricky Skaggs has taken traditional music and made it new, animating it with his tight tenor vocals, razor-sharp instrumentation and a jazzy drive.*

Ricky Skaggs was born in 1954, but he can be seen as a god-father to the New Country movement. His is a young age to be seen as a godfather to anything, but Ricky can also be called a well-seasoned veteran. At the age of seven he performed on television with Flatt and Scruggs, the legendary bluegrass ensemble, and he went on the road with Ralph Stanley of the Stanley Brothers when he was 15.

But it is neither age nor experience that qualifies Ricky for honors as a pathfinder in the revolution that returned country music to its roots: it is his example. In the early 1980s the pop infestation still had Nashville in its grip. Ricky was a rising musician with a wealth of talent, matched only by his ambition. Yet at a time when traditional honky-tonk was a tough sell, he harkened back to deeper roots – mountain music, gospel, bluegrass, high harmonies, sentimental lyrics – and refused to budge. He played old-fashioned music and was amused to see it hailed as new.

A consummate musician, Ricky took old songs and added driving beats and some modern instrumentation, including some electric and some drums. He played traditional music with contemporary pizazz. But he retained the purity of country lyrics and a deep respect for the various country roots of his favored music – the hallmark of New Country.

He was born near Cordell, Kentucky, deep in bluegrass country, deep in traditions of home and church. These themes played a large part in the music of the region. Ricky took to the music as well as to the values, and was a child prodigy on several instruments. In Ricky's late teens he joined several of the "progressive bluegrass" groups that bridged country fans and urban audiences, that sought to meld bluegrass, country, rock, folk and even jazz: the Country Gentlemen, J.D. Crowe and the New South, his own Boone Creek ensemble. He toured to rural shows and college festivals, and recorded for regional labels like Sugar Hill. Ricky's awesome abilities and versatility

Left: *Ricky Skaggs is infrequently seen in repose, as he is here, relaxing on his touring bus.*

Below: *Ricky is a dynamo in concert, playing several instruments – including banjo, fiddle and mandolin – in the course of feverish performances.*

Bottom and right: *With his trademark sound, Ricky has "come home to stay" in New Country. Spirituality is a strong component in his life and music; he thanked Jesus at his CMA sweep, and has performed on television's "700 Club."*

led to his joining Emmylou Harris's Hot Band (succeeding Rodney Crowell); his encyclopedic familiarity with many classic traditionalist tunes led directly to Emmylou's landmark acoustical and roots-oriented album *Roses in the Snow*.

After his classic *Sweet Temptations* album was released on Sugar Hill amidst critical acclaim and sidework by the likes of Emmylou, Bobby Hicks and Albert Lee, Ricky was offered an Epic Records contract. *Waitin' for the Sun to Shine* was his first Nashville album, and "Don't Get Above Your Raising" – a jazzy, uptempo cover of the Flatt and Scruggs classic – was its surprise hit single. Two other singles, "Crying My Heart Out Over You" and "I Don't Care," were number one hits. In fact Ricky scored invariably with hit albums and singles (including "Uncle Pen," the first solo bluegrass number one in "Billboard" lists since 1949) until he hit a bump in the road with his 1987 album *Love's Gonna Get Ya*, which was too rock 'n' roll for his fans' taste. He followed with *Comin' Home To Stay* and apologized to fans for straying from the neo-traditionalist paths he helped forge.

Along the way Ricky picked up honors from his peers: Top New Male Vocalist (Academy of Country Music, 1981); Horizon Award (Country Music Association, 1982); Star of Tomorrow (Music City News, 1983); Male Vocalist of the Year (CMA, 1982); Vocal Duo of the Year (CMA, 1987, with his wife Sharon of the Whites, a country-bluegrass group with whom he had once played); many instrumentalist honors and three Grammy awards; and 1985 CMA Entertainer of the Year.

It is Ricky's confidence in his abilities and taste that allows him to produce Dolly Parton's *White Limozeen* roots-oriented album, or invite Elvis Costello to jam on stage with him in London, or produce a video of his "Country Boy" hit starring Bill Monroe dancing on a subway train and Mayor Ed Koch lip-synching bluegrass, or run his own publishing company and booking office. Ricky Skaggs uses all his resources to pay homage to his values and his heritage. We call his style New Country, but Ricky knows it as what has been there, and been good, all the time.

# George Strait

Right: *Straight-shooting George Strait revives the traditional sounds of country music ballads, western swing and honky-tonk.*

Right: *In his quiet way – with impressive talent and impeccable performances – George Strait connects with audiences in his concerts.*

Of those superstars whose egos aren't as big as their tour buses, some are modest; some are private; some are painfully shy despite the demands of their type of work; some simply think their lives beyond records and stage shows are nobody's business but their own. The reclusive George Strait displays all these tendencies, but mostly he is a down-home, nononsense, regular guy, that's all. A regular guy who possesses enormous talent and a quiet but fierce determination to do what he wants. And what he has wanted to do in the music business – in the face of initial advice to the contrary – is revive and relive the traditional sounds of country music ballads, western swing, and jivin' honky-tonk. In that quiet way he was one of the precursors of the New Country resurgence, and remains one of its kings.

If there is a passion George enjoys as much as his music, it is life on the soil and with his horses and cattle. He was born (in Poteet, Texas, and reared in nearby Pearsall) into a ranching environment; he maintains today a large cattle ranch; and he organizes an annual Roping Classic. Among his unfulfilled dreams – it's actually still a goal – is to compete at rodeo-prize levels in roping.

George received a bachelor's degree in agriculture. Music was peripheral to him when growing up ("My father didn't even have a phonograph"), but after learning the guitar from a Hank Williams songbook, he played with a garage-band of rock 'n' roller high school friends, and fronted a country band while with the army in Hawaii. The interest in country music continued when in college, where he advertised on a bulletin board as a singer in search of a band. A group called the Ace in the Hole Band made contact, and he joined as lead singer. Today the band remains his back-up group.

After college he ran the family's 1,000-head cattle farm, but at night played local Texas dates, singing western swing in the style of idols like Bob Wills, and traditionalist country in the style of Merle Haggard and George Jones. He recorded some songs for "Pappy" Dailey, the man who gave George Jones his start and guidance many years before, to modest regional notice. Another Texan, Erv Woolsey, who ran a San Marcos nightclub that frequently hosted the Ace in the Hole Band, also saw promise in George. However, Woolsey had more current connections, especially when he became an executive with MCA Records.

Woolsey arranged a recording contract, and the result – George's first national album, *Strait Country* – produced an immediate Top Ten hit, "Unwound." The song was a traditional Texas two-step dance number, and while there may have been some residual novelty in such music from the "Urban Cowboy" craze, George Strait was different. His music was reverential, not gimmicky; it was authentic, not exploitative; it was honest and it was fun. And it was embraced. The variety of George's material – from ballads to up-tempo swing, carried by his smooth baritone – has propelled nearly 30 consecutive number one hits, the most prominent of which have been "Ace in the Hole," "All My Ex's Live in Texas," "Does Fort Worth Ever Cross Your Mind," "You Look So Good in Love," "Ocean Front Property," "Love With End, Amen," and "Famous Last Words of a Fool."

Among the many tokens of recognition George has received are consecutive awards: Top Male Vocalist from the Academy of Country Music in 1984 and '85, and from the Country Music Association in 1985 and '86; Entertainer of the Year from the CMA in 1989 and '90. George won the same award from the ACM in 1989.

After his daughter's tragic death in an auto accident in 1986, George became even more reclusive, especially from interviewers. But he has been known to slip into clubs incognito to keep in touch with current tastes, and he has maintained his performance schedule (breaking ticket-sale records, for instance, at the Astrodome). The reviewer Ken Tucker once wrote of George's ability to go through an entire concert without breaking a sweat, purportedly a criticism of the singer's lack of passion. George does indeed reflect his laid-back personality in his performance, seldom talking or telling jokes, but there is no question of his passion for his music – straight-up and traditional.

Above right: *With multiple awards in top male vocalist and entertainer of the year categories, George has exhibited as much staying power as talent.*

Right: *George overcame the public's perception of his obsessive shyness with an impressive acting performance in the 1992 motion picture* True Country.

# Marty Stuart

Left: *Not just a singer/ songwriter reviving quality forms of the past, Marty Stuart is also an enthusiastic fan of country music. He owns a Hank Williams guitar, Ernest Tubb's touring bus, and a closet full of rhinestone-studded suits and jackets.*

If there were an embodiment of the phrase "new traditionalist" it would be the person who is Marty Stuart. He is a New Country star conscious of country-music roots, who has played with some of the most influential gospel, bluegrass, rockabilly and country acts. He reveres that upbringing, and he maintains the traditions.

Marty was born in Philadelphia, Mississippi, and showed an early aptitude for music. At the age of 12 he was hired to play mandolin with the Sullivan Family gospel group that played in the bluegrass style. A year later Marty's proficiency on the instrument led him to Lester Flatt's touring group. The legendary master of bluegrass took Marty under his wing as they toured for about eight years. After Lester's death in 1979 Marty played for Johnny Cash six years, joined the "bluegrass fusion" movement with the likes of Vassar Clements, and recorded a couple of albums – *Marty, With a Little Help from My Friends*, self-recorded on Ridge Runner Records, and *Busy Bee Cafe* on the regional Sugar Hill label. Nashville was taking notice, and in the mid-1980s Marty recorded a couple of albums for Columbia, but only one was released and poor promotion temporarily interrupted Marty's rise.

He returned to Mississippi to take stock of his roots, and to rejoin the Sullivan Family. Then, readjusted, he returned to Nashville. Marty signed with MCA Records and almost immediately took off like a rocket with his first albums *Hillbilly Rock*; *Tempted*; and *This One's Gonna Hurt You*. "The Whiskey Ain't Working" was a number one single, a duet with Travis Tritt off the latter's album; "This One's Gonna Hurt You (For a Long, Long Time)" was a Tritt collaboration off Marty's album. This song received notice as the freshest New Country activity in years. The pair received the "Vocal Event" Award from the Country Music Association in 1992. In a sense, Marty Stuart has joined country music legends; it's where he wants to be and where he belongs.

# Pam Tillis

Right: *Stories of the young Pam Tillis sleeping in her famous father's guitar case at performances are true, but Pam's ascent to country music stardom has been strictly on her own merits.*

Below: *Pam Tillis is a free spirit who displays that spirit in lively concert performances.*

Merely her father's daughter? Singer/songwriter Pam Tillis for years ran from her famous father's shadow – and ran from country music too. But when she returned to country she commanded respect and even awe.

Pam's father is Mel Tillis, one of the greatest country music songwriters in history, a comedian, an actor and an acclaimed singer. Such a father is easily a dominating presence in a youngster's life if the youngster tries to follow the same callings. But the truth is that Mel wasn't much of a physical presence in Pam's life. Pam grew up a troubled teen, the victim of a car crash that left her face horribly disfigured, an experimenter with musical styles that ranged from disco to punk. And not much country.

But recordings and performances yielded Pam little success. She eventually moved back to Nashville, becoming a session singer and a songwriter. Her compositions began to garner attention – stars like Ricky Van Shelton and Highway 101 had notable hits with her songs – and she was signed as a singer by Arista Records in 1990. "Don't Tell Me What To Do," the single release from her first album *Put Yourself in My Place*, shot to number one on music charts. The song by Pam, who by now was known as Nashville's free spirit, was nominated as the Country Music Association's Single of the Year in 1991, and "Maybe It Was Memphis," a follow-up hit single, was nominated in the same category the next year. In the same two years Pam was nominated by the CMA for the Horizon Award, but she has

already come over the horizon and is a prominent part of the New Country.

The best approximation of Pam Tillis's singing style and stage persona is a line from her autobiographical song "Melancholy Child": "You take some black Irish temper and some solemn Cherokee, a southern sense of humor and you got someone like me."

# Aaron Tippin

Right: *A talented singer/ songwriter and an award-winning bodybuilder, Aaron Tippin muscled his way into New Country fans' hearts with his animated concerts.*

Below: *Aaron Tippin demonstrates his intensity on stage – an intense dedication to country forms.*

The intensity of Aaron Tippin's animated stage performances comes through on his records. If Aaron is a "new traditionalist" – and he is indeed at the forefront of the New Country crowd – then his emphasis is on traditionalism. Others hearken back to rockabilly and honky-tonk singers, but Aaron's heavy accents, wide vocal arcs, and blues flavorings recall country music legends like Jimmie Rodgers.

Aaron was born in Pensacola, Florida, and was reared in Greenville, South Carolina (where he recently taped a highly rated performance video, *There Ain't Nothin' Wrong With the Radio*). He started playing guitar at 10 and grew up splitting his dreams between country music – he performed with local bluegrass and country bands – and aviation. The energy crisis of the early 1980s helped decide his course. He moved to Nashville, but acceptance was slow; he worked a graveyard-shift factory job in Kentucky and drove regularly to Music City to pitch his songs. Finally he became a staff writer at Acuff-Rose, where he also sang on his own demos.

RCA picked Tippin up, and his first album, *You've Got To Stand For Something*, was a striking success. The title song, a hit single, was drenched in traditionalist country sounds, but the lyrics spoke of a sensitized individualism, a potent combination that brought strong reactions from fans. His albums are filled with intense, soulful, country purity. His follow-up to *You've Got To Stand For Something* was the acclaimed hit album *Read Between the Lines*.

# Randy Travis

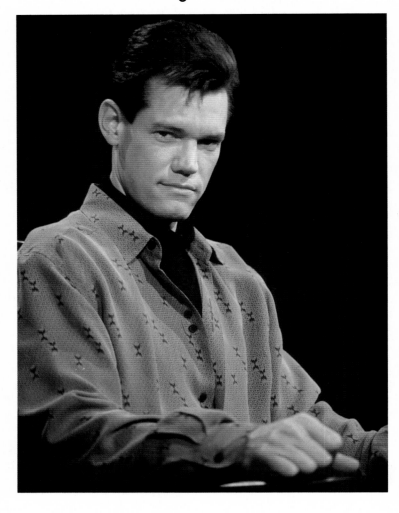

Right: *Randy Travis maintained his sound and stylings during country's fling with pop music during the eighties, and eventually the world caught up with him. His debut album went platinum, demonstrating the popularity of traditional country.*

Right: *Randy Travis, disciple and prophet of New Country.*

It can be argued that one man changed the pop trend in country during the eighties, embodying the change that we call New Country, and his name is Randy Travis. The story of his period of struggle manifests the rigid mindset against the traditional sounds that he resurrected. Randy never changed his voice, his sound or his stylings, yet he was ignored and passed over for years until he prevailed. The world caught up with him; he did not change to suit passing fads. And when the world *did* catch up with him, it discovered that he simply and proudly maintained the best of country music's traditions, which – Randy Travis or no Randy Travis – were there all along.

Born Randy Traywick in North Carolina, by the time he was 17 in 1966 he had pursued his two main avocations with equal zeal: country music and brushes with the law. He was facing a possible five-year term for breaking and entering at the time he won a talent contest at the Country City USA honky-tonk in Charlotte. The club's manager, Lib Hatcher, persuaded the judge to grant Randy probation in her care. Hatcher became Randy's manager (her husband eventually filed for divorce, and she eventually married her young protege) and

the pair soon moved to Nashville. He performed as Randy Ray, working his way up from cook to singer in a club Hatcher managed, the Nashville Palace. Singer Joe Stampley produced several songs for Randy on a small label, with little notice. Members of the Music City establishment heard Randy sing many times, but whether he was on stage or on demo tapes, he was rejected. His sound was simply considered too outmoded and traditional.

Finally Warner Bros. (which had previously rejected Randy) took a flyer, and new producer Kyle Lehning put together the album *Storms of Life*. The Travis sound caught on: the record was the first-ever in country music to go platinum as a debut album, and it spent 12 weeks as number one on country album charts. Randy picked up a host of awards from the major country music organizations (as well as Grammy awards), and was invited to join the Grand Ole Opry. Then came his second album, *Always and Forever*, which left the success of the first in the dust: it was number one on album charts for 10 months, and established Randy as a superstar who was more than a flash in the pan.

Left: *Randy's shy demeanor masks a fierce determination in his life and music.*

Below left: *Randy with wife and mentor Lib Hatcher, who aided Randy's rise in clubs in North Carolina and Nashville, and has managed his contracts and appearances.*

Below and right: *When Randy first hit Nashville (as Randy Ray) no one took notice; he presumably sounded too much like Lefty and Merle. In New Country today – thanks in large part to Randy Travis – no one can sound enough like Lefty or Merle.*

74

Above: *Randy with Kenny Rogers. It was with another Rogers (Roy), as well as with Loretta Lynn, Conway Twitty, Vern Gosdin, Merle Haggard, George Jones and others, with whom Randy recorded a tribute album to his heroes and friends.*

His shy demeanor, country good looks, and smooth back-of-the-throat, crack-in-the-voice baritone put Randy squarely in the tradition of Lefty Frizzell and Merle Haggard. So much has changed in country music since he introduced the changes that he is sometimes thought of as an old-timer; but even though his career is well shorter than a decade, he can take the success of those who followed in his wake, the many other New Country stars, in stride. His self-assurance, in fact, led to his recording a tribute/duets album (*Heroes and Friends*) with such old-timers as Merle Haggard, George Jones and Roy Rogers. And this acclaimed album, like Randy's whole career, has given true country fans a reason to turn pessimism into optimism about the future of the music they love.

# Travis Tritt

Right: *Bluegrass and blue-collar influences play a part in Travis Tritt's music, which includes lively working-class anthems.*

Right: *Travis Tritt on sacred ground, on the stage of the Grand Ole Opry, where he is one of the many New Country stars headlining the new generation in the footsteps of Roy Acuff and Hank Williams.*

Not all the stars in the New Country constellation hearken back to honky-tonk heroes of mainstream country. Travis Tritt is a singer whose early love of music by southern rockers like the Allman Brothers, Lynyrd Skynyrd, and the Marshall Tucker band – as well as that of Merle Haggard and George Jones, to be sure – formed his musical identity. But his taste was formed by a rejection of the pop influences of the early 1980s, so the solid varieties of no-nonsense country led Travis to a slightly different tradition than that of the "new traditionalists," but squarely in a tradition nonetheless. In a puckish declaration of independence from the mainstream and western swing country stars like Garth Brooks, George Strait and Alan Jackson, Travis and friend Marty Stuart went on the road as the "No Hats Tour" in 1992.

But it should be remembered that Marty had played for years with Lester Flatt's bluegrass ensemble, and Travis was reared on bluegrass too; so all the influences are there, and New Country is one big, multi-faceted family.

Travis was born James Travis Tritt in Marietta, Georgia, and grew up singing his first performances as soloist in his church choir. He taught himself guitar at age eight and wrote his first song at the age of 14. His parents divorced but later re-married, and Travis worked in various blue-collar jobs. All these experiences have been reflected in his work (and his personal life; Travis has already been married and divorced twice) – writing and singing heartache songs and working-class anthems.

While working in little clubs throughout Georgia, Travis was discovered by a local Warner Bros. representative, Danny Davenport, who encouraged the singer/songwriter's talent and helped him record demos. The tapes led to a contract with Warner Bros. (who tried unsuccessfully to get Travis to change at least his first name; they had Randy Travis under contract already), and also resulted in Ken Kragen signing on as his manager. Kragen manages Kenny Rogers, among others, and was the organizer of the "We Are the World" and "Hands Across America" events. Travis's talent, coupled with a major-label deal and Kragen's clout, assured the singer's rise.

Travis's debut album was 1990's *Country Club*. Containing a mix of southern rock and hard-driven traditional country, it was certified platinum in just more than a year. The follow-up album, *It's All About to Change*, yielded four number one singles and zoomed to double-platinum status. If Travis has a trademark song, it might be that album's sassy catch-

phrase single, "Here's a Quarter (Call Someone Who Cares)." Travis's third album, *t-r-o-u-b-l-e*, features a rowdy blue-collar battle-song, "Lord Have Mercy On the Working Man." This song couldn't be more traditionally country, with its dobros, driving guitars, and a background chorus that includes George Jones, Tanya Tucker, Porter Wagoner, T. Graham Brown, Brooks and Dunn, and Little Texas. Another cut from the album, a jab at a certain class of preachers, "Bible Belt," was used in the soundtrack of the 1992 movie *My Cousin Vinnie*. Travis's cover of an Elvis Presley song, "Burnin' Love," is heard in the motion picture *Honeymoon in Vegas*. Reflecting the two strains of influences that make up the music of Travis Tritt, on the same day in May of 1991 he performed southern rock at Charlie Daniels's Volunteer Jam, and that night was inducted as the youngest member of the Grand Ole Opry. Travis was a nominee for the Country Music Association's Male Vocalist of the Year and Entertainer of the Year awards in 1992; his song "Here's a Quarter (Call Someone Who Cares)" was nominated for Song of the Year; and he and Marty Stuart of the No Hats Tour won the Vocal Event category award. Travis thanked the CMA by video hookup from Texas, where he was filming a TV movie with Kenny Rogers, *Rio Diablo*.

Top: *Travis is a freewheeling soul whose shoot-from-the-lip remarks sometimes make waves – like his alleged disparagement of Billy Ray Cyrus ("A misunderstanding," says Travis).*

Above: *A star of 1992's "No Hats Tour" with Marty Stuart, Travis has no prejudice against other forms of country, and his outfits have become trademarks.*

# Tanya Tucker

Right: *Tanya Tucker, who has survived, prevailed, and triumphed in country music.*

Below: *Having recorded five Top Ten albums by the tender age of 16, Tanya Tucker is a veteran performer.*

There probably is no entertainer in this book to whom the "new" in New Country is more appropriately applied than Tanya Tucker. She performs new material with as much verve and integrity as traditionalist numbers; she's enjoying a second – or third – career in country music after forays into rock music and a hiatus due to personal problems; and she always is the center of a new controversy, the most recent being her unwed-mothering of two lovely children.

Tanya is only in her mid-30s but has had enough hits, honors and *living* to fill anyone else's long career. Born in Seminole, Texas, she was urged into show business, and into country music, by her parents. Delores Taylor, a Presley song-writer who had discovered Johnny Rivers, sent Tanya to Billy Sherrill at Columbia/Epic records.

One of Tanya's trademarks is a husky, sultry voice wrapped around adult, often suggestive lyrics. This is some-times controversial today, but was an anomaly in the industry of 1972, when Tanya was 13 and she charted with "Delta Dawn." Her follow-ups through the years were equally as provocative – "Blood Red and Going Down," "Would You Lay with Me in a Field of Stone," "What's Your Mama's Name," "The Man That Turned My Mama On" – until she ventured into rock music in the late 1970s. Tanya's career went cold as she largely abandoned her country base. In the early 1980s, reportedly close to broke, and after several publicized affairs (including an ill-starred engagement to Glen Campbell), she was absent from recording sessions for several years.

*Left: Tanya with members of the Nitty Gritty Dirt Band.*

*Right: At home with rockin' dance tunes and mournful ballads – and everything in between – Tanya is a consummate singer.*

*Below left: Tanya's sexy image and individualist ways have marked her from her teen debut through adulthood.*

*Below: Tanya with her daughter, Presley (the name would have been given to her child, Tanya says, even if the child had been a boy).*

*Above and right: No shrinking violet, Tanya has used her incredible energy and talent to propel her to the forefront of New Country. She is one of two performers in this book to have had hits since the early 1970s (the other is across the page), but she constantly stays in the forefront of new sounds and contemporary tastes.*

Tanya emerged in 1986 with a Capitol (now Liberty Records) contract. And true to form for country music fans, her audience awaited and was pleased to hear a re-dedication to country music.

In truth Tanya had not completely left country: many of her rock releases were backed with country songs, and her "middle period" saw some of her finest country tunes, including "San Antonio Stroll," "Don't Believe My Heart Can Stand Another You," "A Cowboy-Lovin' Night," "Pecos Promenade," and "Texas (When I Die)." Another bump in the road occurred in 1988, when Tanya checked into the Betty Ford clinic for alcohol and cocaine dependency. The same year, however, saw her real return to country music prominence. She had a hit album with *Love Me Like You Used To*, and a single, "I Won't Take Less

Than Your Love" (recorded with songwriters Paul Overstreet and Paul Davis), had a solid traditionalist theme. Since 1988 Tanya has been nominated for many awards, from the Country Music Association, the Academy of Country Music, Music City News, and the Grammies. For three years in a row she was nominated by the CMA as Top Female Vocalist; she won the award in 1991, the night her son Beau (brother to daughter Presley) was born.

Tanya can still rock with anyone in the New Country – her 1992 cut with bluesman Delbert McClinton, "Tell Me About It," is proof enough (100 proof) – but she is comfortable, too, with country roots, as demonstrated by her rendition of the 1920s country classic, Jimmie Rodgers's "Daddy and Home," on her *Strong Enough to Bend* album.

# Jerry Jeff Walker

Left: *One of the most literate of New Country's risk-takers, Jerry Jeff Walker produces a body of work rather than a succession of songs.*

He's over 50 years old and has been making music since the 1960s, yet he's arguably one of the most innovative and interesting of the artists in New Country. He's a country singer but started in rock and folk. He is one of the leaders of the "Austin Sound" – a guru to the progressive country, Luckenbach-mystique, Texas-connection movements – yet he was born in New York State. He is made up of varied influences, unpredictable styles, constant experimentations, and a country commitment. He's Jerry Jeff Walker.

He was born Ronald Clyde Crosby in Oneonta, New York, in 1942. He grew up on folk and rock, traveled the country, sang in clubs and on the street, and met a dancer named Bojangles in 1965 in the New Orleans First Precinct Jail. The character inspired the classic song that memorably has been performed by groups and singers from the Nitty Gritty Dirt Band to Sammy Davis Jr. to Jerry Jeff himself. He became Jerry Jeff Walker in 1966, and the following year formed the Lost Sea Dreamers which became the house band at Manhattan's Electric Circus; the band changed its name to Circus Maximus and recorded two albums. A spinoff hit, still a classic in various styles, was "Wind." When Circus Maximus split up, Jerry Jeff Walker recorded and performed as a solo act, at the Newport Folk Festival and, eventually, in the Austin area.

Austin has been the other side of the mirror to Nashville through the years. The Austin mystique was recognized by the early 1970s as a magnet for creative musicians. Jerry Jeff brought several things to Texas stages and recording studios: a comfortable familiarity with country, rock and folk music; an array of East Coast musicians to cross-pollinate with Texas traditionalists and rockers; a genius for writing story-songs that meshed with a new generation of musical poets who were also drawn to Austin. Between 1972 and 1982, on albums for MCA and Elektra/Asylum, he and his Lost Gonzo Band or the Bandito Band experimented with rowdy anthems and tender love songs, road ballads and home calls in such releases as "Viva Terlingua" (recorded live at the Luckenbach Dance Hall), "A Man Must Carry On," "Too Old To Change," and "Cowjazz." His ensemble's recording of Gary P. Nunn's "London Homesick Blues" became the theme song for the long-running television concert series "Austin City Limits," where Jerry Jeff frequently has appeared. In 1991 Jerry Jeff began hosting "The Texas Connection" on the Nashville Network, interviewing and playing with fellow artists.

In 1986 Jerry Jeff and his wife Susan formed their independent record label, Tried & True Music, for Jerry Jeff's releases and those of proteges like Chris Wall. Singles from that

Above and right: *Jerry Jeff Walker has travelled many roads – from New York to Austin, from rock to folk to country, from Circus Maximus to Mr. Bojangles to Luckenbach. He is so identified with the progressive Austin Sound that he hosts TV's "Texas Connection" each week.*

Below: *Jerry Jeff is an important leader of a significant strain of New Country.*

partnership have included hits like "Pickup Truck Song," "I Feel Like Hank Williams Tonight," "Time To Stay Home," and "Tonight I Fell in Love Again." Many of Jerry Jeff's recent albums have been recorded live or from sessions in his den. Although the 1992 album *Hill Country Rain* was a disciplined, and quality, return to studio standards, Jerry Jeff is at his best in concert – exercising a musical free-association, careening from style to style. His voice, similarly, ranges from weathered growls and shouts to velvet balladry.

On his albums Jerry Jeff still records the songs of such old Texan and New Country songwriters as Guy Clark, Don Schlitz and Steve Fromholz. But he still is a songwriter himself of awesome sensitivity and electric moods. The fact that he frequently re-records his classics too is testament to the fact that he is not merely a tunesmith; Jerry Jeff has a view of life, with its wildness, its humor, its precious moments, that he examines and re-examines.

# Michelle Wright

Right: *Michelle Wright's songs explore unique points of view and exhibit the singer's masterful versatility.*

Below: *An exciting performer is the Canadian ambassador of New Country, Michelle Wright.*

Canada has always had a strong country music following, and it is unfortunate that the U.S. has not been more open to it. Through the years there have been many quality performers in English and French, and now there is the Canadian Country Music Association. And there is Michelle Wright, a Canadian who has scored on U.S. country charts.

Michelle was born in Chatham and grew up in Merlin, small Ontario farming communities. Her parents performed country music locally. So did Michelle, right after high school graduation, and she released her first album in 1988. Songwriter Rick Giles saw her performing in Ontario and beckoned her to Nashville, where she became one of the first artists signed by Arista Records. Although little-known in the U.S., Michelle was by then a substantial star in her native country, having won multiple awards from the Canadian Country Music Association, including Female Vocalist of the Year.

Her first U.S. album (1991) was self-titled and yielded the hit single "New Kind of Love." Her second, *Now and Then*, featured the title song "Take It Like Man," and "One Time Around." Michelle sings with a heartfelt passion in all her songs, which tend to be more about life than just love affairs. She brings emotional credentials to typical real-life country lyrics: her parents split when she was a child, and she is a recovering alcoholic.

Michelle has toured with Randy Travis, Alabama, the Nitty Gritty Dirt Band, and on the Marlboro Music Military Tour to U.S. bases. Transferring her success from Canada to the U.S., she may give a new definition to the term "crossover."

# Wynonna

Right: *Born in Kentucky, Wynonna grew up in Los Angeles, and achieved her first number one single, with mother Naomi, in 1984.*

Below and right: *No longer just her momma's girl, Wynonna now stands alone in the spotlight. Her first solo album,* Wynonna, *assured her future success.*

Through the years many country music stars have split off from groups and established their own successful solo careers. But featured singers who split with their partners in groups have not always been assured of successful solo careers. Wynonna Judd appears to be breaking that mold. After more than seven successful years with her mother, Naomi, as The Judds, Wy went on her own in 1992. Naomi retired, she said, for health reasons. Amidst great publicity and a lengthy farewell tour, The Judds finally did split up, and Wy's first solo was eagerly anticipated.

The Judd family (Naomi's real name is Diana; Wynonna's is Christina) had moved from Kentucky to Hollywood back to Kentucky while Naomi, a single mother, raised her daughters always close to, and trying to break into, show business. (Naomi's other daughter, Ashley, returned to Hollywood, where she became a star of the television series "Sisters.") Back around Nashville, where Naomi worked at jobs, including nursing and modeling, demo tapes by her and her daughter were heard by RCA executives, who signed the singers to a contract. Almost immediately, in 1983, they charted with several major hit singles, which have included "Had A Dream," "Mama He's

Above: *Wynonna plays guitar and struts onstage during her elaborate performances, sometimes wearing a head-mike a la Garth Brooks.*

Right: *Naomi Judd with daughter Wynonna – the most-awarded duo in country music in the 1980s. Naomi has retired for the present.*

Crazy," "Grandpa," "Change of Heart," "Guardian Angels" and "Love Can Build a Bridge." All of their albums turned gold, and several have been certified platinum. Many awards followed their Horizon Award from the Country Music Association in 1984, including Grammies, and consecutive Vocal Duet awards from the CMA (1985-1991) and Vocal Duo from the Academy of Country Music (1984-1991).

As mother and daughter they sang a wide range of country music, and the stretches closer to driving rock seemed to be more of Wy's preference, with her throaty vocals and growls. (Growing up in California, she recalls, her favorite music included West Coast rock bands; and even as a country star she reportedly immersed herself in the music of Tracy Chapman and Bonnie Raitt.) Naomi and Wynonna frequently displayed tension on stage, and Wy's headstrong tendencies might move her solo career in new directions. Her successful debut album *Wynonna* spun off the hit singles "She Is His Only Need" and "No One Else on Earth"; Naomi came out of retirement to sing harmony on "When I Reach the Place I'm Goin'" and cowrote (with the hot Mike Reid) the cut "My Strongest Weakness."

# Trisha Yearwood

Right: *Trisha Yearwood gained recognition with help from Garth Brooks, but gained fame on the strength of her uniquely emotive voice.*

Below: *Two of the biggest-selling female contemporary country singers: Trisha Yearwood (left) and Reba McEntire.*

A tall blonde singer from Monticello, Georgia, burst onto the country music scene in 1991, with a little help from her friends. Trisha Yearwood had made a pact with Garth Brooks a few years earlier when they were both struggling, vowing that the first one to achieve success would then boost the other's career. Garth hit it big and invited Trisha to be his roadshow opening act. Trisha was also helped by experience gained in Nashville as a music business student at Belmont University, as an intern in the publicity department of a record label, and as a receptionist at a record company. But Trisha's best attribute is her voice – one of the clearest and most emotive in Music City, one that Garth Brooks said "could sell oil to the Arabs."

Actually the enabling link that turned Trisha from hopeful to professional is a job that has emerged from the shadows in recent years, that of demo singer. Executives around Nashville started noticing Trisha's vocals instead of the songs, and her career took off. Veteran producer Garth Fundis recommended her to MCA Records, and handled her studio session when she signed a contract. Her first album, self-titled, was a smash hit, and its first single, "She's In Love With the Boy," shot to number one. The album was also aided by a strong contingent of writers (including two by Garth Brooks) and side-

Above: *Trisha Yearwood has become one of the most versatile and popular of New Country's acts. She has recorded with, opened for, and toured with the biggest of today's stars, and has achieved major stardom herself.*

Right: *Trisha started out in Nashville as a publicity intern, receptionist and demo singer. Her number one debut single, "She's in Love with the Boy," established her as a promising new voice in New Country.*

Left: *Trisha poses with country legend Johnny Cash.*

90

men (Brooks and Vince Gill on harmony; rock musician Al Kooper on organ). Trisha's vocal idol is Linda Ronstadt, and her boss is her own sense of direction. (Nashville was abuzz in late 1992 about her decision to join Randy Travis's tour and drop Garth Brooks's management team, falsely citing a friendship rift instead of Trisha's independence.) Her identity is unique; she has a propensity to choose lyrics that reflect a man's point of view about love (songs often written for men) to invite her fans to consider roles and points of view.

*Above: Trisha Yearwood at the 1992 Aids Project Los Angeles Benefit. The talented newcomer performed at the Country Music Association Awards. One of country's leading ladies, Trisha has reached the same plateau as two singers who have inspired her most: Linda Ronstadt and Reba McEntire.*

Trisha was nominated for both the Horizon Award and Female Vocalist of the Year in 1992 by the Country Music Association; she performed "Walk Away Joe" on the telecast, with Don Henley joining her for harmony in a surprise that delighted the audience.

# Dwight Yoakam

Left: *Best-known for his own brand of hillbilly music – encompassing bluegrass, western swing, honky-tonk and string band music – Dwight Yoakam has helped revitalize country music with a new spin on old forms.*

"Revivalist" is a term in country music circles that once referred only to evangelical camp-meetings; today it often has a different spin, and it is frequently spun around Dwight Yoakam. He revives the music of his youth and his region – of before his time and beyond his area, too – of mountain music, string bands, honky-tonk, the electrified "Bakersfield Sound," rockabilly, and hard-edged, twangy, road-house country ballads of the '50s. Spurned in Nashville for "sounding too country" during the pop infestation, he is now a conduit for the old sounds and new expressions that combine these days to make up the New Country movement. Like a true believer at a revivalist service, Dwight never doubted.

He doesn't revive classic material in the form of a novelty, like Patsy Montana attending rodeos; neither does he resurrect old songs note for note. Dwight Yoakam – with trademark torn jeans and a perpetual scowl under his low-slung western hat – seems country-punk in the backlot sense of that word. A kind of rockin' chip-on-his-shoulder country music is his brand, celebrated with brassy vocals, twangy guitars, screaming steels and driving beats.

Born in Pikeville, Kentucky, and reared in Columbus,

Ohio, by a gas station owner, his musical influences were then as they are now: Hank Williams, Bill Monroe and honky-tonk. He grew up singing Ralph Stanley style bluegrass, and his first band was rockabilly. It was in the mid-seventies when Dwight first tried his hand at Nashville and was rebuffed. He was in his twenties, and astonished that the home of country music would be counseling against traditional country sounds. He retreated to Los Angeles but not from his standards, and plotted an interesting route: having a strong feel for the connection between late honky-tonk and early rock 'n' roll, Dwight hit the rock scene with his hard-driving country music. Rather than continue the Nashville debate in country bars, he thought, he would take his driving rockabilly to rock clubs and, if necessary, turn things up several notches to get accepted. He was, and it helped that the L.A. music scene was into "roots" and authentic sounds at the time, for it granted an imprimatur to Dwight's hard-edged music and electronically echoing tenor vocals. He graduated from acceptance to cult status.

Dwight cut a song for the first of the innovative *Town South of Bakersfield* series of albums; it was heard by producer Pete Anderson, and together the pair recorded a mini-album,

Left and right: *Dwight Yoakam is one of the most exciting of New Country's performers, recalling the twangy electric sounds of the 1950s' Bakersfield Movement. He is a "new traditionalist" in a different tradition than others.*

Below: *Despite his image as a rebel, Dwight is not only a friendly sort but seeks out the company of industry legends, whether it's the Bakersfield icon Buck Owens or Nashville's own Minnie Pearl.*

*Cadillacs, Guitars, Etc., Etc.*, which made its way to Warner Bros./Reprise executives. Finally Dwight was just country enough for Nashville. The mini-album was beefed up with more cuts and released with the same title to great acclaim. The album, which has been certified platinum, saw its first hit single as a revival of Johnny Horton's rockabilly classic, "Honky Tonk Man." Indeed through his subsequent albums (*Hillbilly Deluxe*, *Buenas Noches From a Lonely Room*, and *If There Was a Way*) there has been a peppering of updated versions of old hits of Stonewall Jackson, Lefty Frizzell, Gram Parsons (the legendary "Sin City," sung in duet with k.d. lang), and Buck Owens. Buck Owens has been an icon to Dwight, and he walked into Buck's Bakersfield office unannounced one afternoon. A friendship developed; Dwight drew his idol back into the recording studio for duets ("Streets of Bakersfield"), for a concert tour, and, ultimately, for a brief, two-album Buck Owens renaissance on his old label Capitol.

*Buenas Noches* had veered toward introspection, somewhat of a new direction for Dwight, although the old sounds were still reincarnated in him. *If There Was a Way* was an album that returned to the purer musical fun of his first sessions. One cut was "Send a Message to My Heart," a duet with Patty Loveless; "It Only Hurts When I Cry" was cowritten with legendary singer/songwriter Roger Miller (the first collaboration for either artist). Lucas Films produced the video for another of the album's songs, "Turn It On, Turn It Up, Turn Me Loose."

Dwight was named Top New Male Vocalist (1986) and won the Vocal Collaboration Award with Buck Owens (1989) from the West Coast-based Academy of Country Music, but has no awards from Nashville's Country Music Association. It is widely supposed that, although Dwight frequently visits Music City, the Nashville establishment still resents some remarks by Dwight about their practices, standards . . . and timing.

# Index

## PHOTO CREDITS

Atlantic Records: 46 top
Country Music Foundation: 7 top, 8 top right and bottom left, 9 all three
Jeff Frazier: 35
Ron Galella Ltd/Albert Ortega: 30, 33
Globe Photos Inc.: 86 bottom. John Barrett: 31, 32. Ralph Dominguez: 14 left, 15 bottom, 29 bottom, 47, 48 both, 52, 53 top, 60, 62 bottom, 68 bottom, 74 bottom left, 93. Jonathan Green: 39 top. Lynn McAfee: 79 bottom, 81. Lisa Rose: 13 bottom, 25 top, 34 bottom, 36 bottom, 78 bottom, 80 bottom left. Adam Scull: 14 right, 42 top, 79 top.
Ron Keith: 34 top
Rick Marschall: 84 top
© Alan L. Mayor: 10 bottom, 16 bottom, 19, 21, 24 top, 45 bottom, 70 bottom, 71 bottom, 85 bottom, 86 top
Scott Newton/Austin City Limits: 15 top, 27, 45 top, 58 bottom, 69, 70 top
Scott Newton/Texas Connection: 46 bottom, 84 bottom left and right
Frank Ockenfels: 71 top
Retna Limited: Jay Blakesberg: 17, 64 bottom right. Adrian Buckmaster: 85 top. Larry Busacca: 12, 40 left, 63. Camacho Stills: 74 top left. Donna Driesel: 55, 59 top, 76. Peter Figen: 88 top. Gary Gershoff: 13 top, 22 top, 23, 42 bottom, 82 right. Steve Granitz: 11, 18 bottom, 20, 75 right, 90 top, 92, 95. Beth Gwinn: 1, 4, 7 bottom, 8 bottom right, 16 top, 18 top, 24 bottom, 25 bottom, 28 bottom, 29 bottom, 36 top, 37 bottom, 38 both, 39 bottom, 40 right, 43, 44 both, 49, 50, 53 bottom, 56 both, 58 top, 64 top left, 67, 73, 74 right, 75 top left, 77, 78 top, 80 top and bottom right, 86 bottom, 89 bottom, 90 bottom, 91, 94 top and bottom. Robert Matheu: 28 top, 94 middle. Lynn McAfee: 82. Frank Micelotta: 87. Daniel Root: 72, 89 top. Susan Rutman: 41, 68 top. Bill Schwab: 2, 22 bottom, 26, 54, 57, 64 top right, 65.
Evelyn Shriver Agency: 61, 62 top
Sony Music Publicity: 37 top, 59 bottom
Titley Quinn: 51
Scott van Osdol: 83
Warner Bros. Records: 10 top
The Erv Woodsey Co.: 66